Amish Agriculture in Iowa: Indigenous Knowledge for Sustainable Small-Farm Systems

By

Rhonda Lou Yoder

Center for Indigenous Knowledge for Agriculture and Rural Development
Iowa State University

Studies in Technology and Social Change, No. 15

Technology and Social Change Program
Iowa State University
Ames, Iowa 50011 USA

in collaboration with

The Leiden Ethnosystems And Development Programme (LEAD)
Institute of Cultural and Social Studies
University of Leiden
P. O. Box 9555
2300 RB Leiden, The Netherlands

© 1990, Iowa State University Research Foundation
ISSN 0896-1905
ISBN 0-945271-24-7

Printed in The Netherlands

Amish Agriculture in Iowa: Indigenous Knowledge for Sustainable Small-Farm Systems

This study has been supported by public and private non-profit organizations. All or part of this publication may be reproduced in any form or by any means. Citation of the source will be appreciated.

This project was funded by FORD FOUNDATION, CONACYT, Colegio de Postgraduados, and Iowa State University. Support for printing this monograph was provided by LEAD, University of Leiden.

TABLE OF CONTENTS

	Page
ACKNOWLEDGMENTS	iv
CHAPTER ONE: SETTING THE STAGE	1
Introduction	1
Issues	2
Water	2
Land stewardship	2
Alternatives	3
The Wisdom of Farmers	4
The Old Order Amish	7
Summary	8
CHAPTER TWO: HISTORICAL DEVELOPMENT	11
Introduction	11
European Development	11
Movement to the United States	14
The Iowa Experience	17
Contemporary Characteristics	18
Summary	20
CHAPTER THREE: METHODS	22
Introduction	22
Definitions	22
The farming system	22
Ethnoscience	23
Culture	23
Cognitive anthropology	24
Cultural relevance	24
Farmer-centered research	24
Indigenous knowledge systems	25
Framework	25
Procedures	26
Presentation of Data	28
Summary	29
CHAPTER FOUR: FINDINGS AND DISCUSSION	31
Introduction	31
Practice	32
Introduction	32
Discussion: Inputs	33
Predicaments	35
Introduction	35
Discussion: Continuity and change	36
Philosophy	37
Introduction	37
Discussion: Values and agriculture	38
Cultural Patterns	40
Introduction	40
Discussion: Social organization and agriculture	41
Summary	42

CHAPTER FIVE: CONCLUSIONS AND RECOMMENDATIONS 46
    Introduction 46
    Key Characteristics 46
        Scale 46
        Farm operation 46
        Cropping patterns 47
        External inputs 47
        Support systems 47
    Underlying Beliefs 47
        Agrarian life 47
        Ethics 48
        The community 48
    Indicators of Success 48
        Stability and productivity 48
        Production costs 49
        Soil conservation and environmental protection .. 50
    The Amish and Sustainable Agriculture 50
        Introduction 50
        The limitations of the Amish system 50
        The lessons of Amish agriculture 52
        Applying the lessons of Amish agriculture 53
    Summary and Recommendations 54
        Introduction 54
        Research 54
        Policy 56
        Conclusion 57
BIBLIOGRAPHY 58
LIST OF PARTICIPANTS 69

ACKNOWLEDGMENTS

The author wishes to thank the Leopold Center for Sustainable Agriculture at Iowa State University for the research grant they made available for the support of this study. Special thanks are also due to the many participants who so generously shared their time and experience with the author, and to the author's family who provided encouragement and support throughout the process. Finally, the author is indebted to Kirsten Klassen for her insightful editorial comments.

CHAPTER ONE: SETTING THE STAGE

Introduction

In recent years, the structure of agriculture in Iowa has changed dramatically. During the past forty years, farmers have become increasingly dependent on high inputs of commercial fertilizer, pesticides, heavy machinery and fossil fuel. But the methods of farming are not the only things to have changed. During this same time period, farm numbers have fallen sharply and average farm size has increased. In Iowa, a fifty percent decrease in the number of farms occurred between 1950 and 1990, while average farm size increased by approximately fifty percent (Fruhling 1989; Iowa Agricultural Statistics et al. 1989). These changes have dramatically altered the rural landscape.

Numerous factors have been attributed to this change process: farming methods (e.g., mechanization), public policy (including farm support programs) and variability in the macro-economic environment. From the economic boom of the early 1970s, to the farm crisis of the 1980s, Iowa's farmers have risen and fallen. The effects of the crisis in agriculture were not limited to farmers, however. Iowa also lost numerous banks, grocery stores, farm implement dealerships, Main Street businesses and citizens.

> During the '80s, after the big bust in farming, Iowa's economy grew at only half the pace of the national economy and significantly more slowly than the economies of neighboring Missouri, Minnesota, Nebraska and Illinois. ... By the time the hardship had begun to ease, Iowa had become a far different place. There were 39 fewer banks, 27 fewer savings and loan associations, 458 fewer grocery stores, 257 fewer automobile dealers, 1,458 fewer gas stations, and, worst of all, 80,000 fewer people (Fruhling 1989, 9 and 1).

Iowa's rural areas, and the state as a whole, suffered a tremendous blow as residents and their resources departed (1).

Along with this complex boom and bust cycle has come the realization that agriculture has more than economic problems. As Iowa was losing businesses, farms, farmers and other residents, Iowa was also losing topsoil. Since 1950, as more and more land has been planted to corn and soybeans and farming patterns have changed from diversified to specialized systems, soil erosion has increased (Soil Conservation Service 1986). The irony in this situation is that for the past fifty years federal and state government programs have focused on promoting soil conservation. Conventional practices, such as the continuous cultivation of a single crop, and farm programs, by encouraging these practices and making high production the primary goal, have worked against soil conservation efforts (Committee on the Role of Alternative Farming Methods in Modern Production Agriculture 1989).

The long-term effects of soil erosion and groundwater pollution to the natural environment, and the effects of agricultural practices on food safety and public health, are now central issues which stir heated debate. For example, in a recent issue of _Iowa Farmer Today_, a front page headline read, "Environment dominating farm debate" (Christopher 1990). This is not uncommon. In recent months, many articles have appeared that explore the relationship of conventional farming methods and current environmental concerns.

Issues

Water

One of the major topics in Iowa has been, and continues to be, the contamination of surface and groundwater supplies. Although the extent of the problem is unclear and the exact implications remain to be seen, it is definitely a cause for concern. Kelly et al. (n.d., 22) report that extensive, low-level pesticide contamination is being uncovered in Iowa's groundwater and that "there is still a great deal that is not known about how pesticides behave in the environment and what threat they may pose to human health." In 1986, a report from the Iowa Department of Natural Resources stated that "the most commonly used pesticides are now routinely detected in the state's primary source of drinking water. Recent investigations suggest that over 25 percent of the state's population is now exposed to pesticides through consumption of their drinking water" (Kelley 1986, 1). Another report indicates that "in Iowa, 27 of the 33 public water supplies from surface water sources tested, or 82 percent, had 2 or more pesticides detected in treated drinking water samples; 73 percent had 3 or more; 58 percent had 4 or more; and 21 percent had 5 or more" (Committee on the Role of Alternative Farming 1989, 101).

Water supply contamination is not limited to Iowa, of course. It is occurring in many parts of the United States. Areas which depend heavily on agriculture are likely to be among the first and most adversely affected because "agriculture is the largest single nonpoint source of water pollutants, including sediments, salts, fertilizers, pesticides, and manures. ... In at least 26 states, some pesticides have found their way into groundwater as a result of normal agricultural practice" (Committee on the Role of Alternative Farming 1989, 89).

In 1987, the Iowa legislature passed the Groundwater Protection Act, a law which provides money for research at Iowa's three regent's universities and establishes revenues to encourage recycling, groundwater education and mapping of groundwater supplies in Iowa (Leonard 1989). More importantly, perhaps, passage of this law brings sustainable agriculture off of the back burner and into a place of priority. This reflects the desire to develop a new ethical and environmental consciousness among Iowa's citizens (Deibert & Malia 1988).

Land stewardship

There is now a growing recognition that land stewardship, an ethical orientation, is as essential to farming as is the soil itself. The Iowa-born conservationist, Aldo Leopold, recognized the necessity for land stewardship many years ago. In the foreword to <u>Sand County Almanac</u> (Leopold 1984, xviii-xix), he wrote: "We abuse land because we regard it as a commodity belonging to us. When we see land as a community to which we belong, we may begin to use it with love and respect." Leopold outlined the need he saw for a land ethic -- a way of living which respects and cares for the land.

As the need for land stewardship has been increasingly recognized, the need to modify conventional agricultural practices, which have become destructive to the natural environment, has also become clear. This has led to the current emphasis on sustainable agriculture (for example, Francis, Flora and King 1990; Edwards et al. 1990).

When the Iowa legislature passed the Groundwater Protection Act, sustainable agriculture was defined as "the appropriate use of crop and livestock systems and agricultural inputs supporting those activities which maintain economic and social viability while preserving the high productivity and quality of Iowa's land (Iowa Legislature 1987, 39). Deibert and Malia (1988, 5) defined sustainable agriculture as "a way of production that will return a consistent profit to the producer, be less harmful to the environment and to personal health, and provide a basis for a sustainable community by offering a way for people to stay on the land and be less dependent on federal payments for their livelihood." These definitions emphasize economic, social and environmental components, all of which are essential for long-term sustainability.

Alternatives

Ten years ago, sustainable, regenerative and organic agriculture were phrases and practices patently ignored or treated with disdain in conventional circles. With the publication of Report and Recommendations on Organic Farming by the United States Department of Agriculture (USDA) Study Team on Organic Farming (1980), a gradual shift began to occur. A quick look at current newspaper, magazine and radio reports reveals that alternative agriculture is now a frequently discussed topic. In the 27 January 1990 edition of Iowa Farmer Today, for example, a new series on sustainable agriculture was unveiled. Sustainable agriculture is also being discussed by agricultural researchers, economists and policy makers. According to a report in the South Bend Tribune (Falda 1988b), "The upheaval of U.S. agriculture combined with growing doubts among Americans over widespread use of pesticides on their food have given regenerative agriculture a new image of plausibility."

Although the 1980 USDA report on organic farming admitted that "one of the major challenges to agriculture in this decade will be to develop farming systems that can produce the necessary quantity and quality of food and fiber without adversely affecting our soil resources and the environment" (USDA Study Team on Organic Farming 1980, v), it appears that this admonition is only now beginning to be taken seriously. The road to recognition has not been an easy one, nor has it been forged by public institutions or government agencies. The case for sustainable agriculture, which is finally being looked at by these agencies, has basically been pushed by farmers themselves and citizens interested in environmental issues (Soth 1989).

Even though the USDA commissioned and published this early report on organic farming, it also dismissed a member of the study team which produced the report (Soth 1989; Anthan 1989). Additionally, "agribusiness and other big-farming interests have laughed at the new-farm movement labeling it unscientific and a retreat to the inefficient technology of our great-grandfathers" (Soth 1989, 10). Interestingly, it has been farmers themselves, and private, often non-profit, groups such as the Center for Rural Affairs, Rodale Institute and the Institute for Alternative Agriculture, who have advanced the cause of sustainable agriculture (Soth 1989; Anthan 1989).

In Iowa, for example, the Iowa Citizens for Community Improvement, a non-profit organization, published Farming with Fewer Chemicals: A Farmer to Farmer Directory, a handbook describing the farm operations of a number of Iowa farmers who have cut back on the use of nitrogen fertilizers and pesticides (Iowa CCI 1989). A group of Iowa farmers concerned with the development of "environmentally sound, lower cost, profitable farming techniques" (Practical Farmers of Iowa, 2) have organized themselves into a group called Practical Farmers of Iowa. They carry out research, conduct field tours of on-farm demonstrations, hold meetings to discuss pertinent issues, publish a newsletter and provide information to people interested in alternatives to the conventional methods that have contributed to the current crisis in agriculture. As Anthan (1989) reports, it is "farmers themselves who are becoming increasingly concerned over the health and environmental impact of their methods, and skeptical over the long-term economic benefits derived from producing huge quantities of commodities at low prices."

At the national level, a research report entitled <u>Alternative Agriculture</u> was published in 1989 by the National Research Council. The report recognizes that "many agricultural practices have an off-farm impact on society and the environment" and that because of changes in the structure of agriculture and the adverse environmental consequences associated with conventional practices, "many farmers have begun to adopt alternative practices with the goals of reducing input cost, preserving the resource base, and protecting human health" (Committee on the Role of Alternative Farming 1989, 16 and 3). This study examines alternative farming systems currently being used in the United States, provides a background to the current agricultural situation and makes recommendations for the future.

In Iowa, the 1987 Groundwater Protection Act established and appropriated funding for the Leopold Center for Sustainable Agriculture at Iowa State University, the state's primary agricultural research institution. The provisions for the Leopold Center were spelled out in section 266.39 of the <u>Iowa Code</u> (General Assembly of Iowa 1989, 1826-1827). The Center is charged with carrying out research and educational programs related to the development and promotion of sustainable agricultural practices. Specifically, "its goals are to develop and promote agricultural systems that combine responsible stewardship of natural resources with farm profitability" (Leopold Center, 3).

The Wisdom of Farmers

While sustainable agriculture and environmental protection are important issues to be addressed in the '90s, careful attention must be paid to the approaches taken in the quest for responses to these issues. Typically, research at state-supported institutions has been carried out by scientists and then handed down to farmers. Often, research has been funded by private sources (e.g. chemical companies), carried out in isolation from the complex set of factors which operate on a farm and has focused on a single component of the farm system. In practice, this approach has come to mean the transfer of technology (Chambers 1988). In addition, this process has largely ignored the contributions of farmers, their successes and the answers they have already put into practice. As a result, research has often provided very few practical benefits for farmers -- especially for those interested in alternatives to the conventional system. If appropriate responses to current issues are to be developed, farmers must be considered experts in their own right, and their innovations taken seriously and included in the research process.

In the transfer of technology model, farmers are seen primarily as passive recipients of information. However, farmers in all parts of the world are actively and continually experimenting (Rhoades 1987; Chambers 1988; Yoder 1989). Most conventional research has not recognized this fact, nor has it considered the possibility of learning from or utilizing farmers' solutions. Farming systems research (FSR) has acknowledged that research should begin with farmers, learn about farmers' realities, do on-farm experiments and use farmers' criteria to evaluate the results. However, it still assumes that outside experts are the primary participants, and that in comparison, farmers are relatively inactive onlookers (Shaner et al. 1982). Robert Chambers, an internationally-recognized, rural development expert, suggests that "the role of the outsider is to encourage and support analysis by farmers themselves" (1988, 11). Technical scientists are certainly needed to examine various issues and carry out basic research, but the ability of farmers to solve many of their own problems must be affirmed and researchers should be willing to learn from farmers' experience.

The <u>Report and Recommendations on Organic Farming</u> and <u>Alternative Agriculture</u> both acknowledge that farmers have developed ways of farming which are innovative and practical, but they do not directly address the importance of taking the experience of farmers seriously. Altieri (1983) suggests that farmers' knowledge is viewed as "backward" because it has arisen outside mainstream research and extension. Although it has often been overlooked, ignored and labeled as irrelevant, the "indigenous knowledge" of farmers represents a valuable resource which should be explored.

Refusing to take this knowledge seriously results in lost opportunities, misguided efforts and, at times, the introduction of potentially harmful and inappropriate "innovations." According to Warren and Cashman (1988, 8):

> By dismissing indigenous knowledge as irrelevant, rural people may be encouraged to adopt practices that lead to undesirable effects through the inappropriate use of local resources. The new techniques adopted may also undermine the delicate balance of the local cultural or natural environment, causing declines in social welfare. Or the technologies may have little consequence, apart from the wasted expense of time and money involved in developing and extending them.

Whatever the effects, appropriate responses are more likely to be developed with indigenous knowledge than without it.

One of the disturbing results of the farm crisis has been the loss of cultural knowledge. The decline in the farm population means that valuable agricultural knowledge is being lost as farmers lose their farms and leave their rural communities (Jackson 1985). This knowledge cannot be quickly replaced because it has accumulated over many generations and has been adapted to the specific environment in which it was being used. As Arizpe (1988, 18) says, "Knowledge is the backbone of a culture: if this is undermined, the whole social fabric of that culture will slowly fall apart." It is exactly this kind of indigenous agricultural knowledge which is now needed. As Wendell Berry (1989, 1) has pointed out in a 1988 Iowa Humanities Lecture on the theme "A Sense of Place: Small Towns, Community, and the Land":

> A human community, then, if it is to last long, must exert a sort of centripetal force, holding local soil and local memory in place. ... As local community decays along with local economy, a kind of vast amnesia settles over the countryside. As the exposed and disregarded soil departs with the rains, so local knowledge and local memory move away to the cities, or are forgotten under the influence of homogenized sales talk, entertainment and education.

Not only does knowledge leave when farmers leave, the loss of cultural knowledge contributes to the overall decay of rural areas.

Indeed, many rural communities which depended on the existence of family farming are now dead or in the process of dying. Historically, family farming has been assumed to be the ideal model for American agriculture. As Strange (1988, 1) points out, "perhaps no part of our cultural life is more widely approved of in America." But those left on the farm and in rural communities face an uncertain and unpredictable future. The crisis in agriculture has called attention to the social and economic instability in rural communities, as thousands of farm families have been forced out of farming. Additionally, economists and other public officials often paint a grim picture for the future of family farming. In an article entitled "Agricultural Research Policy and the Family Farm," Adler (1989, 2) has this to say:

> According to the Congressional Office of Technology Assessment (OTA), the total number of farms - including the family farm - will continue its historical decline from 2.2 million in 1982 to 1.2 million in 2000. By the turn of the century, only about 1 million small and part-time farms (80%) will remain in existence, with the largest third of the projected 175,000 large and very large farms (14.0%) accounting for over 75% of annual agricultural production. Small farms, *i.e.*, those having less than $100,000 in sales, 'are not viable economic entities in the mainstream of commercial agriculture - nor can they be made so.' Moderate size farms, *i.e.*, the 'family' farm, having annual sales from $100,000-$250,000, will decrease in number by more than half from 180,000 to 75,000 during this period.

Similarly, economists at an Agribusiness Outlook and Policy Conference held in Des Moines, Iowa, in February of 1989 predicted that "the demise of family farms is inevitable if U.S. farmers want to remain competitive in the international market" (Gillete 1989).

Rural areas of the United States have historically been prone to economic vulnerability, and because of the current decline in rural population the nations's farmers and rural residents are losing representation (Christopher 1990). Because they are a dispersed minority, rural residents have little political influence (Jackson 1989). In addition, as pointed out earlier, farmers are typically stereotyped as country bumpkins and are given little respect for the knowledge and experience they possess. Farmers are also often viewed as the primary culprits responsible for environmental degradation. These circumstances, combined with the current interest in sustainable agriculture, leave Iowa's farmers faced with a challenge.

As appropriate responses to the current social, economic and environmental issues of agriculture are searched for, there are two basic issues to keep in mind. First, solutions which ignore the desires, experience and priorities of farmers will be difficult to implement and maintain, and may be inappropriate or destructive. Second, although the understanding and wisdom of farmers is often ridiculed and viewed as unscientific (Otto and Burns 1981; Altieri 1983), an untapped reservoir of ideas and solutions already exists in farming systems which have maintained themselves over the years. There are some farmers who have weathered the storms. Unfortunately, though, the knowledge of these "survivors" has been consistently overlooked. One of the purposes of this study is to examine a system that seems to be working, and to explore the knowledge and values upon which it is based.

Instead of starting from scratch, we have the opportunity to observe the long-term effects of some alternative practices as they already exist on successful farms. While examining existing solutions has been advocated for use at the international level (Chambers 1983; Richards 1985; Brokensha et al. 1980), very little attention has been paid to its application in the United States.

The Old Order Amish

In Iowa, one farming system which appears to be relatively successful, socially, economically and environmentally, but which has not been adequately understood, is that of the Old Order Amish. The Amish (2) have been farming in Iowa for nearly 150 years and have developed an amazingly stable farming system. A quick look at the Amish in Iowa suggests that, according to external standards, the Amish could be classified as successful because they (1) have kept themselves on the farm during the decline in farm population (Erb 1985); (2) apply lower rates of commercial fertilizers and pesticides (Erb 1987; Participant 5); (3) tend to depend heavily on renewable energy -- animal traction and wind power, for example -- rather than on high levels of petroleum-based energy; and (4) produce much of their own food supply in addition to marketing agricultural products such as milk, hogs and beef cattle (Yoder 1989).

Given their unique position in Iowa agriculture, the experience and knowledge of Amish farmers represent a valuable resource for others interested in stable, sustainable farming systems. Although some have called the Amish way of life something which is "long since obsolete" (Doak 1983), their persistence on the Iowa landscape is testimony to the relevance and endurance of their ways. As Olshan (1980, 174) points out, the Old Order Amish "represent an on-going community where a wealth of experience and information is accumulated." It is ironic, then, that this thriving subculture is viewed as irrelevant when it is one of the few active and growing small-farm systems left in the state. Perhaps the rest of Iowa can learn something from the Amish.

Although many studies have looked at various aspects of Amish life (for example, Hostetler 1980a; Cronk 1977; Getz 1946a and 1946b; Huntington 1956; Kollmorgen 1942; Kraybill 1989; Meyers 1983b; Nagata 1968; Olshan 1980; Schwieder and Schwieder 1975; and Yutzy 1961), relatively few have focused specifically on Amish agricultural practices (Biggs 1981; Craumer 1977; Jackson 1988; LeCompte 1984). Recently, a number of popular articles have appeared about Amish agriculture (Hoard's Dairyman 1989; Erb 1985, 1987, 1988; Falda 1988a; Logsdon 1986, 1988, 1988,1989; Schneider 1986; Stone 1989; Weidner 1988). Very few of the studies or popular articles, however, have examined the Amish in Iowa.

The states most commonly represented are Pennsylvania, Ohio and Indiana, the three states with the largest Amish population (Luthy 1985). Because Iowa's Amish are fewer in number, they have often been overlooked.

To provide information relevant to the current agricultural scene in Iowa, this report aims to summarize some of what is known about Amish agriculture in Iowa. The current study is not a technical report, but rather a summary of descriptive information obtained from available written sources and from first-hand observations of and participation in an Amish community. Along with outlining specific agricultural practices, this study is also concerned with identifying the values which underlie these practices. According to Redfield and Warner (1940, 986), "Each society has built up through the past and present experiences of its members, including their relations with individuals of their own and other groups, a way of life which regulates the lives of the individuals in it and gives these individuals a set of values by which they live." Understanding a way of life different from one's own and the values which maintain that way of life is an essential means of reflecting on one's own life. Learning from others may enable our society to move beyond its own current limits.

Summary

Given the problems associated with conventional agriculture and the current interest in more sustainable farming systems, it is necessary to identify elements which may be helpful in establishing a new, alternative system. The study of agriculture among the Amish was carried out to test the hypothesis that Amish agriculture in Iowa represents a model of sustainable agriculture. If this is true, people outside of the Amish system who are interested in alternative agriculture can then learn from the Amish example and modify and apply some of these practices in their own systems. Perhaps the least this study can do is encourage understanding, respect and tolerance of and for those who have chosen to remain outside of mainstream American culture and agriculture. Even if there were no possible benefits to be derived from this study, the resilience of the Amish farming system alone is enough to merit further exploration and analysis.

Some of the questions to be discussed in this report include: What makes Amish farmers unique?; In what ways are Amish farmers similar to other Iowa farmers?; What elements characterize Amish agriculture?; How have the Amish managed to maintain their small scale of agriculture when modern-day farmers are supposed to "get big or get out"?; How has the current agricultural reality affected Amish farmers?; and, How does the social organization of the Amish community affect farming practices and the decisions which are made about agriculture?

The Amish provide an interesting departure from conventional agriculture. This is especially noteworthy since the Amish seem to have been one of the most resilient groups during the farm crisis. They have maintained their family farming patterns, have retained nearly one hundred percent of their land holdings and have been productive without high levels of external inputs. Their practices also appear to be highly sustainable over a long period of time, something the agricultural community and the public in Iowa are interested in because of issues such as groundwater pollution, soil erosion and the demise of rural communities. The stability of the Old Order Amish farming system in Iowa is something the rest of Iowa may do well to learn from.

Notes

1. It appears that these trends had begun to turn around by 1990.

2. The Old Order Amish are only one of several groups who can properly be called Amish. In this report, however, the terms Amish, Old Order and Old Order Amish will all be used to refer to the contemporary Old Order Amish. If this pattern is broken, the exception will be noted in the text.

CHAPTER TWO: HISTORICAL DEVELOPMENT

Introduction

The subjects of this study, the Old Order Amish of Iowa, have a rather complicated history, but it is important to understand this history if one wants to comprehend their current situation. In this chapter, an overview of Old Order history will be presented to provide a context from which to make a more accurate interpretation of the study data. The discussion will be divided into European Development, Movement to the United States, The Iowa Experience and Contemporary Characteristics, some information about the current demographic status and social organization of the Old Order Amish.

European Development

The story of the Old Order Amish began in central Europe during the tumultuous religious upheaval of the early 1500s. This upheaval, commonly referred to as the Protestant Reformation, challenged the authority of the Catholic Church, which had become wedded to the dominant political system and operated as the official state religion in much of Europe. At this time, the religious system and the political system were, practically speaking, a single entity. Membership in the Catholic Church was ensured by requiring all infants born in Catholic territory to be baptized into the Catholic Church. This also assured the state a means of control over its citizens (Bender 1942; Estep 1975; Hostetler 1980a).

Although individuals and small groups had rebelled against this system since its inception, the most serious challenge followed Martin Luther's campaign of dissent, which began in 1517. Protestant reformers such as Luther, John Calvin and Ulrich Zwingli departed from the Catholic Church, but did not break totally with the established church-state system and retained many Catholic religious traditions. Areas which adopted the new Protestantism became Protestant states. The Catholic Church struggled against this shift in power and

> thus began a great conflict which lasted over a hundred years, 1521-1648. During the latter part of this struggle the Catholic countries of Europe engaged in a great war of extermination against the Protestant countries. This war, lasting from 1618-1648, has been known as the Thirty Years' War. In the end neither side won, both sides agreeing in 1648 to mutual toleration (Bender 1942, 13).

Even as the Catholics and Protestants were fighting each other, they were also unified in their opposition to a third movement.

In the early stages of the Protestant Reformation, some reformers were not satisfied with the compromises made by those who chose to retain parts of the church-state system. These reformers wanted to form a church based on voluntary, adult membership, which would be autonomous from the state. These people began to practice adult baptism among themselves, appointed their own ministers and were consequently labeled as Anabaptists, meaning re-baptizers, by their opponents. They also refused to have their infant children baptized into either state church, Catholic or Protestant. According to Wenger (1947, 167), "...for the Anabaptists it was impossible to accept the idea of a provincial church which embraced the entire population of the land.... The only people the Anabaptists could consider members of the church were those who had made a personal commitment to Christ."

In Zurich, Switzerland, Ulrich Zwingli led a movement which became the Reformed Church. Some of Zwingli's students wanted to make more radical changes than Zwingli and the ruling town council would allow. In January, 1525, some of those who were dissatisfied with the Reformed Church in Zurich baptized themselves as adults and formed their own group. These Anabaptist reformers called themselves Brethren. "Since there were Brethren in various places in Europe in the course of the following years, it soon became the custom to refer to the ones who first founded the church in Switzerland as the Swiss Brethren" (Bender 1942, 14-15). Because they were viewed as a threat to the established order of both the Catholics and the Protestants, they were put in prison, tortured, killed and banished from certain areas. In Switzerland, the Brethren were not fully tolerated until 1815 (Bender 1942; Wenger 1947).

The Swiss Brethren were not the only Anabaptists or even the sole originators of the Anabaptist movement. Other Anabaptist groups, who began independently of the Swiss Brethren, were also present in other areas of central and northern Europe (Stayer et al. 1975; Smith 1909). At one time or another, there were, however, descendents and converts of the Swiss Brethren in other cantons of Switzerland, and in Austria, Tyrol, Alsace, Montbéliard, Lorraine, Bavaria and the Palatinate, for example (Bender 1942; Wenger 1947).

In 1534, Dutch Anabaptism was founded by Obbe Philips. In 1536, Philips baptized Menno Simons, a former Catholic priest, who then became an outstanding leader among the Dutch Anabaptists. By 1544, the Dutch Brethren were being called Mennists, after Menno Simons (Wenger 1947; Bender 1942). Eventually, these Brethren became known as Mennonites, a term which was subsequently used for all the Brethren. Like their counterparts in Switzerland, the Dutch Brethren were also persecuted, but they were informally tolerated many years before the Swiss Brethren were granted legal toleration.

During their formative years in Europe, many Swiss Brethren became farmers or developed other forms of rural employment. Because their religious activities were illegal, they were often banished from certain areas, including villages, and were forced to live in remote, rural and often mountainous regions. "Relentless persecution of the Swiss Taüfer (sic) had compelled them to find refuge on the least accessible plains and in the mountains. ...large congregations either began in or moved to inhospitable and fairly sterile areas where livestock farming and the creation of an imaginative agriculture became necessary for survival" (Séguy 1973, 182).

Wenger (1947) uses 1641 as the year Swiss Brethren from Berne and Zurich began to move to the Vosges Mountains of Alsace to escape the severe persecution by Swiss authorities. During the seventeenth century, other Swiss Brethren went to Lorraine, the Palatinate and the Netherlands (Hostetler 1955). At the beginning of the eighteenth century, some of the Swiss Brethren settlers in Alsace moved on to an area of south Germany, Montbéliard, Zweibrucken and the Palatinate because an attempt was made to drive them out of Alsace (Wenger 1947).

Although the Swiss Brethren were restricted from living in certain areas, they were originally permitted to live in Alsace because there was a shortage of farm labor in that region (Séguy 1973). Meyers (1983b) suggests that in addition to religious reasons, which are invoked the most often, this indicates the significance of socio-political factors in decisions to move.

In many places the Swiss Brethren were not permitted to own land. In 1531, for example, Landgraf Philip of Hesse issued a regulation which included the requirement that those who had been baptized as adults, even those who had not preached for the movement, must sell their land and property. Thereafter, they were not allowed to own land in territory under his authority (Hege 1931). Even in Alsace, where they were initially permitted to live, they "were forbidden by law to purchase land" until after the Revolution of 1789 (Séguy 1973, 223). This prohibition against land ownership was one of the factors which motivated the Swiss Brethren to develop innovative agricultural practices (Séguy 1973; Meyers 1983b; Hostetler 1980a; Kollmorgen 1942). Because they could not own land, the Brethren often reinvested their earnings in cattle (beef and dairy), hogs and sheep, and, consequently, they developed new approaches to integrated crop and livestock farming (Séguy 1973). This is an approach to farming which sets their descendents apart even today.

Meyers (1983b) suggests that a combination of religious values and structural factors are responsible for the agricultural success of the Swiss Brethren.

> Part of the reason that they were among the leading group of innovators in agriculture in 17th and 18th century Europe can be attributed to the fact that: (1) They had large families which provided them with an important source of labor; (2) because of their religion they were prohibited to marry outside of the faith; (3) they were prohibited from owning land and thus had to live outside of villages; (4) and finally without a land base they were forced to turn to animal husbandry (50-51).

Both Séguy (1973) and Meyers (1983b) point out that ministers and young men who were seeking wives may have traveled between the scattered congregations and thus spread information about their agricultural ideas through these visits. This would have helped the Swiss Brethren to develop and diffuse new farming techniques.

The Old Order Amish are primarily the descendents of the Alsatian Swiss Brethren. In the late 1600s, a Swiss Brethren minister from Markirch, Jacob Ammann, began to question his fellow Swiss Brethren ministers in Alsace, the Palatinate and Switzerland to see how they would respond to the standards he believed the group should endorse and enforce. Ammann believed the ministers should demand stricter standards of discipline, specifically, the social avoidance (<u>Meidung</u>) of those who had been excommunicated and that they should institute the practice of footwashing, both of which were included in the Dordrecht Confession of Faith (adopted by Dutch Anabaptists in 1632 in Dort, Holland). Although the Swiss Brethren in Alsace had begun to use the Dordrecht Confession in 1660 (Wenger 1947), the Swiss Brethren in other areas were using the Schleitheim Articles of Faith, which had been adopted by the Swiss Brethren in 1527 in Schleitheim, Switzerland. In 1693, Ammann expelled Swiss Brethren ministers and their congregations from Berne, Alsace and the Palatinate who did not agree with him. In time, those who chose to side with Ammann became known as Amish, or Amish-Mennonites (Wenger 1947; Hostetler 1980a; Bender 1942; Dyck 1967).

Movement to the United States

Severe persecution, the resulting migration and lack of freedom to faithfully carry out the tenets of their faith, such as nonresistance, motivated many Swiss Brethren to seek new homes. Reference has been made to their movement within Europe, which occurred from the beginning of the Anabaptist movement, but eventually the decision was made to move to areas being settled by Europeans in North America. Sometime before 1740 (perhaps as early as the 1720s, but certainly by 1736), the first Amish-Mennonites arrived in what is now eastern Pennsylvania from Switzerland and the Palatinate (MacMaster 1985; Reschly 1987; Wenger 1947; Hostetler 1959). The first Amish congregation (church) in this area was formed around 1740 in present-day Berks County, Pennsylvania (Bender 1934). This first period of immigration, which began in the 1720s or 1730s, lasted through 1770 and consisted of between 500 and 1000 individuals. These early Amish immigrants settled in what are now Berks, Chester, Lancaster and Lebanon counties of Pennsylvania (Reschly 1987; Crowley 1978).

A second wave of Amish emigration from Europe occurred between 1815 and 1860 (Reschly 1987; Hostetler 1959; Wenger 1947). One segment of these Amish emigrants (from Alsace, Bavaria and Montbéliard) formed new communities in Ohio, Illinois, Ontario and Iowa. Another segment (from Waldeck and Hesse-Cassel) settled in western Pennsylvania (Hostetler 1959). Others settled in Indiana, New York and Nebraska (Reschly 1987; Bender 1934). Many Alsatian Amish emigrated at this time because of the "rigid militarism of the French" (Wenger 1947, 155). During this wave, there were between 1500 and 3000 new Amish immigrants (Reschly 1987; Crowley 1978).

Often the Amish immigrants who came to the United States continued to move after their arrival and initial settlement. By the end of the 1700s, for example, two new settlements in central and southwestern Pennsylvania had been formed by people who had originally settled in eastern Pennsylvania. These new settlements were in Mifflin County and Somerset County (Bender 1934; Crowley 1978; Reschly 1987). Later, people from the Somerset County area founded new settlements in Tuscarawas and Holmes counties, Ohio, and some of the Mifflin County settlers moved on to Logan, Champaign and Stark counties, Ohio (Reschly 1987). These new settlements also spawned additional westward movement.

By 1865, the Amish immigrants were in the process of splitting into two main groups, the Amish Mennonites and the Old Order Amish Mennonites (Reschly 1987). Before this time, the term "Old Order" had never been used. As Hostetler (1959, 43) states,

> 'Old Order' Amish is strictly an American term which came into usage as some Amish Mennonite congregations resisted 'new' methods of church work as well as 'new' forms of social organization and technology. One cannot properly speak of 'Old Order' before 1850, and its usage came gradually after about 1870, or following the Amish Ministers' Conference 1862-1878, called <u>Diener versammlungen</u>, which finally crystallized the differences between the more progressive Amish and the Old Order groups.

Thus, the mid-1800s is now known as "The Great Separation" (Bender 1934) or "The Great Schism" (Yoder 1979) in Amish Mennonite history.

Hostetler (1959) identifies the early immigrants to eastern Pennsylvania (1700s) and the European Amish group that settled in western Pennsylvania (1800s) as among those who are ancestors of the present Old Order. The majority of the Amish who emigrated from Alsace, Bavaria and Montbéliard between 1820 and 1860 and some Amish from each of the other waves of emigration joined together as Amish Mennonites, and by 1925 they had merged with the Mennonite Church in the United States and had dropped the name Amish. In total, "about one third of the Amish Mennonites existing in 1850 continued in the Old Order..." (43).

As a result of these various groupings and re-groupings, the terms "Amish" and "Mennonite" are rather confusing. To understand their appropriate meaning, the moment in time and the geographic context of the group in question must be considered. Before 1850, Amish (or Amish-Mennonite) referred to descendents of the Swiss Brethren in Europe and the United States who had followed the direction established by Jacob Ammann after the 1693 division. The Swiss Brethren who did not become Amish in 1693, along with other northern European Anabaptists, became known as Mennonites. As mentioned earlier, the term "Mennonite" had originated among the Dutch Anabaptists. Thus, in the "Old World", the two main groups considered to be the ancestors of current North American Amish (and Mennonites of Amish descent) are the Swiss-German Mennonites and Swiss-German Amish-Mennonites. In the early stages of the Anabaptist movement, the Swiss-German Mennonites and Amish-Mennonites were both part of the Swiss Brethren.

The Amish-Mennonites who remained in Europe gradually assimilated with Mennonite groups (the last doing so in 1937) and thus rendered the term "Amish" obsolete in Europe (Hostetler 1955). By 1925 in the United States, the "new world" Amish Mennonites had joined the Mennonite Church (the Mennonites from Europe had also immigrated to the United States) and had become known as Mennonites. Since the early 1900s, then, the term "Amish" in the United States has been used to describe the Old Order and the various groups which separated from them but did not join the Mennonite Church, such as the Beachy Amish, the Nebraska Amish and the New Order Amish (Hostetler 1980a).

Outside observers may find it difficult to comprehend the many divisions which have occurred in the course of Amish history. One explanation for the divisions may lie in the fact that church authority among the Amish has always been congregational (Schlabach 1988; Bender 1934; Dyck 1967). That is, each congregation is ultimately responsible for its own decisions. No higher authority, such as a conference or synod, dictates what a congregation must do. Although each Amish congregation (known commonly as the church district) establishes its own specific rules for day-to-day living, otherwise known as the Ordnung among the Old Order, the basic religious principles found in the Dordrecht Confession of Faith are followed by all Old Order congregations (Hostetler 1980a). Even though certain practices vary from community to community, the guiding principles are the same. As Schwieder and Schwieder (1975, 90) point out,
> Although there is no overall authority or regulation imposed from the top down, each group clearly recognizes the limits of

>change. To remain in the Old Order group, no compromise or
>modification of major religious beliefs will be tolerated even
>though local customs may vary.

As a result of these patterns, authority among the Old Order is quite decentralized, but operates within a system in which the same general beliefs are understood and followed.

Divisions among the Amish also occurred because "they took their religion seriously" (Guengerich 1984, 29). As members of a free church, the Amish had to take responsibility for their own religious decisions and discipline. Right conduct became an important element of this responsibility, and divisions occurred because the Amish believed the visible church needed to be without spot or blemish (Hostetler 1989a; Dyck 1967). Strict discipline was a way to keep the church pure and strong.

When the Amish moved to the United States, they brought with them the agricultural techniques and practices they had developed in Europe and quickly established their reputation as excellent farmers (MacMaster 1985; Craumer 1977; Kollmorgen 1942; Hostetler 1980a; Landis 1945). Beginning with their appearance in U.S. history, and continuing to the present, the Amish in eastern Pennsylvania have been known as exemplary agriculturalists. Lancaster County, in particular, has often been the case used to demonstrate the attributes of the Amish farmer (Kollmorgen 1942; Schneider 1986; Weidner 1988; Knopp 1946; Gehman 1965; Getz 1946a and 1946b; Kraybill 1989; Loomis 1979; Landis 1945; Hostetler 1980a). Due to the thrift and productivity of the Pennsylvania Germans, including the Amish, this area of Pennsylvania has been known as "The Garden Spot" for many years (Landis 1945; Hostetler 1989b; Kollmorgen 1942).

As mentioned earlier, the Amish in Europe had tenuous status as tenant farmers and had been forced to survive in marginal areas. "As a result the Brethren were among the first in central Europe to experiment with new methods of fertilizing the land, of feeding cattle, and of planting new crops" (Kollmorgen 1942, 18). The Amish were among the early developers of stallfeeding and meadow irrigation. They also grew clover, marketed cheese, built up the soil with manure, used gypsum and lime as soil additives and developed a new cattle breed -- things which the average farmer was not doing at the time (Kollmorgen 1942; Séguy 1973).

In southeastern Pennsylvania, the Amish were among those who implemented such "improved practices as diversified farming, rotation of crops, careful use of barnyard manure, use of lime, and the growing of red clover..." (Kollmorgen 1942, 4). As the Amish moved on to establish new settlements, they continued to rely on variations of these methods which were best suited to the soil, climate and topography in each new area. Even though the dominant farming culture eventually discarded many of these practices, the Amish have continued to use them in Pennsylvania and elsewhere (Hostetler 1980a; Kraybill 1989; Schneider 1986; Berry 1977; Erb 1985, 1987, 1988). Ironically, many of these very practices (such as crop rotations, low external inputs and diversified farming) are now being advocated by proponents of sustainable agriculture (Stinner et al. 1989; Lucht 1990). Today, these practices are being called "new", but the Amish have been using them for several centuries.

Perhaps in part because of their long-standing European agricultural traditions, farming grew to be a sacred occupation for the Amish (Landis 1945; Hostetler 1980a; Kraybill 1989). This was not just any kind of farming, but small-scale, family-operated farming -- the kind that is now assumed to be increasingly impossible to maintain in the United States (Adler 1989; Gillete 1989). For the Amish, the family farm is important because it keeps a person near God, it is the best place to raise a family in the Amish faith and it is an integral part of the Amish tradition of remaining separate from mainstream society, thus allowing the Amish to maintain their family and community integrity (Stoltzfus 1973; Martineau and MacQueen 1977; Hostetler 1980a; LeCompte 1984; Thoreau 1980). Farming is the primary means of ensuring family and community stability as well as cultural continuity. Hostetler (1951, 234) contends that "'faith, farm, and family' are the three chief integrating factors in Amish life."

The Iowa Experience

The first Amish in Iowa settled in Lee County in 1839-1840. They came to Iowa from several counties in Ohio. As the Amish settled in the United States, they gradually moved west, either from older, established settlements, or, during the second period of immigration, directly from Europe. After new settlements were formed, they grew through the birth of offspring and through in-migration from any number of older settlements. Thus, the new settlements in the west became a meld of people from many different areas.

The Lee County Amish settlement did not become permanent because the land they lived on was involved in a legal dispute. Instead of involving themselves in the legal process, many of the Amish chose to move. Henry and Davis counties, Iowa, and areas of Illinois and Missouri were among the new destinations for the Lee County Amish. By 1870, the Amish congregation in Lee County had disappeared (Gingerich 1939).

In 1840, when the first Amish were settling in Lee County, four Amish men from Somerset County, Pennsylvania, traveled through southeast Iowa in search of land for a new settlement. They were impressed with the Johnson County area, but because they heard of illness in this region, they chose instead to settle in Elkhart County, Indiana (Gingerich 1939).

In 1845, the Johnson County area was again explored by two prospective Amish settlers. These two men were from Maryland and Ohio. This time Johnson County was chosen as the appropriate spot, and a settlement was begun in April of 1846. This became the first permanent Amish settlement in Iowa (Gingerich 1939).

The first Amish congregation in Johnson County was organized in 1851 (Guengerich 1929; Swartzendruber 1953). Between 1862 and 1864, this congregation was divided into the Deer Creek district and the Sharon district. Then in 1877, because of an expanding population in the community, these two districts were again divided, this time into Upper and Lower Deer Creek and North and South Sharon (Hershberger 1953; Guengerich 1929). By 1890, Guengerich (1929) estimates that there were forty families, or around 100 members, per district.

At various times during the settlement's history, there were disagreements within and between congregations. In 1864, for example, two church leaders moved away because of conflicts between the new, more conservative settlers and the original settlers. Gingerich (1939, 124) says this incident is "illustrative of many in newly organized Amish churches. By 1860 many Amish churches in America had drifted apart, partly because of the isolation of the different communities." Settlers in a new area had to adapt to ideas and practices which were different than those in their community of origin. As a result, conflict was not unusual when settlers came to newly established communities from many different communities and at different times.

In 1878 or 1879, a small group of Amish in the Johnson County area who had begun meeting on their own removed their membership and began to worship in Henry County, Iowa, forty miles to the south of the Johnson County settlement. Because of the distance, this was not satisfactory. Then, for a time, the group had a minister from Henry County come to them occasionally. This too was unworkable. Eventually, a new minister who had moved into the Johnson County community from Elkhart County, Indiana, but who had not been permitted to preach by the Old Order, met with the group. In 1889, this group and their new minister built the first meetinghouse in the area and established the Union Church. The Union Church was the first new (post-1850) American Amish Mennonite congregation in the area (Gingerich 1939; Hershberger 1953; Guengerich 1929; Guengerich 1984).

Although the Old Order do not worship in church buildings and instead meet in the homes of their members, two Old Order congregations, Upper and Lower Deer Creek, both built meetinghouses in 1890 (Hershberger 1953). In 1913, the Lower Deer Creek congregation left the Old Order and affiliated with the Amish Mennonites. At this time their bishop left the district and joined the South Sharon Old Order district. The Upper Deer Creek district left the Old Order in 1915 to join the Conservative Amish Mennonite Conference, a group which did not want to be Old Order, but which did not want to join the Amish Mennonites either. Their bishop moved to Buchanan County, Iowa, where, in 1914, an Old Order settlement had been started by a few families from the Sharon districts (Hershberger 1953). The Old Order in the present-day Kalona, Iowa, area (Johnson and Washington counties) grew out of the two Sharon districts, which remained with the Old Order. In 1951, there were six Old Order church districts in the Kalona area (Hershberger 1953), while there are now seven Old Order districts which make up the Kalona Amish community (Gingerich 1989).

Contemporary Characteristics

Currently, there are six Old Order communities in Iowa. The cluster of church districts in a contiguous geographic area define each distinct community. Each community may have one or a number of church districts. The community near Kalona and the group in Buchanan County have subsequently been joined by communities (in order of origin) near Milton, Bloomfield, Riceville-McIntire and Edgewood. All of these settlements are in eastern Iowa, with the largest being the one near Kalona.

The situation of the Amish in Iowa also needs to be put into the context of the Old Order as a whole. Currently, the Old Order live in twenty states and one Canadian province (Luthy 1985; Raber 1989). Their population has been growing steadily, from an estimated 8,000 in 1900 (Hostetler 1980b), to around 100,000 in 1987 (Hostetler 1987). The exact population is difficult to estimate because of the high birth rate, frequent mobility (among established communities and to start new communities) and lack of official records. The approximate number of church districts may be known for a given year, for example, but this does not indicate population precisely because membership in a district is by families, not by individuals, and the number of families in a district varies with the age of the settlement and its current state of viability.

The number of settlements and church districts may vary widely in a short time span because new Amish settlements are continually being established and some settlements are usually in decline. For example, between 1975 and 1984, fifteen settlements became extinct, while seventy-one new settlements were formed (Luthy 1985).

The mobility evident throughout Amish history is still common. One of the primary reasons given for the founding of new settlements is the need for more land due to population growth within established communities. An Old Order historian writes that

> with land prices highest in the oldest, largest settlements, cheaper land in other areas is always being sought -- thus the dramatic increase in the number of settlements. That the Amish are rapidly spreading out into new areas is best illustrated by the fact that of the 175 settlements in 1984, seventy percent were founded since 1960...(Luthy 1985, 1).

Along with the need for new farmland, there are a variety of other reasons which affect mobility patterns.

Olshan (1980) gives four reasons which may enter into a decision to move. First, conflicts with state or local authorities over disputed regulations may prompt a move. For example, in Minnesota the conflict over the slow-moving vehicle sign requirement for buggies resulted in a court case (Siewers 1988), and the belief that if the ruling was unfavorable for the Amish, many of the Old Order would leave Minnesota (Participant 7). Second, differences of opinion within a settlement may result in the establishment of a new settlement or a move to another settlement. The precedence for this has been pointed out earlier in this chapter, and it continues to be a factor. Third, the Old Order may move to isolate themselves from the influence of other religious groups. For example, the Plain City, Ohio, Old Order settlement is now extinct because the Old Order moved away when many of their offspring began to join other religious groups in the area (Participant 6; Pollack 1981; Yutzy 1961). Fourth, personal reasons often prompt a move to a new community. These reasons may include a mobile nature or the desire to try something new. Schwieder and Schwieder (1975) also support Olshan's analysis and point out that mobility has allowed a certain amount of flexibility and, therefore, has contributed to stability within Amish society. Moving is one acceptable way of embracing change within Amish society.

Amish social organization consists of four basic components: the household, the church district, the settlement and the affiliation (Hostetler 1980a). An Old Order settlement consists of a number of Old Order households (families) located in the same geographic area. Within this geographic area, also called a community, there is the further distinction of church district. Church district boundaries are laid out geographically and consist of twenty to thirty families, the number who can conveniently hold worship at an Amish farmstead. The church district may also be referred to as a congregation. A community may be composed of one or many church districts. "An affiliation is a group of church districts that have a common discipline and that commune together" (Hostetler 1980a, 97). The affiliation may not necessarily represent a specific, contiguous geographic area, but may include a number of districts from a variety of settlements. Within a large settlement there may be several affiliations.

A frequent misconception about the Amish is that they are communal. The Old Order are community-oriented in that they live near other Old Order families, but they neither isolate themselves completely nor practice communal ownership. Old Order families live on their own farms, which are scattered throughout areas that are also populated with non-Amish farmers. Near the center of the older settlements there may be a large concentration of Amish farms, but on the outskirts of the older communities and in the smaller, newer communities, Amish farms are mixed in with non-Amish farms.

The building blocks of the community are the extended family and the church district. Typically, Amish church officials will speak about the number of families in their districts rather than the number of individual members (Participant 8; Huntington 1956). This is an indication of the central place of the family in Amish society and the effort that is made to discourage individualism. On the farm, the family spends a great deal of time working together, and once children are married, they often return home for visits or work days. Aunts, uncles and cousins may also join together to help a family member with a special project. Often, parents remain on the farm in a "grandpa house" when one of their married children takes over the farm. This means that two, three and sometimes four generations all live on one farm. Each family unit has its own home, but much time is spent together.

Next to the extended family, the church district provides the other most frequent opportunity for interaction. A congregation meets every other Sunday, but people see each other between times because they live near one another and may trade labor or share farm equipment. The congregation is small enough that face-to-face accountability can be maintained. Before each biannual communion service, for example, much time is spent making sure relationships in the congregation are in harmony. These two institutions, the extended family and the congregation, develop and maintain the social ties which bind the community together. Hostetler (1955, 213) says, "The cultural survival of the Amish in America is a function of community groupings." This seems to be true, because the Amish do not exist outside of their geographic and religious communities.

Summary

The foundation which was laid during the Anabaptist movement is still reflected in the lives of the Old Order Amish. For the early Anabaptists, church became a community reality, with face-to-face relationships and corporate discipline as core components. These were some of the issues at stake during the 1693 division. With this and other historical factors in mind, one can better understand the current principles, values and social organization of the Old Order.

Understanding Amish history is also of critical importance because of the common belief that the current Old Order way of life simply represents "living history." To many outsiders, Amish culture appears relatively unchanged and unchanging. The Old Order seem to have emphasized the necessity of maintaining the traditions of earlier generations, but a close examination of their history will also reveal that they have made selective accommodations to the broader society in which they live (Meyers 1983a; Olshan 1981; Hostetler 1987; Stoltzfus 1977). Change has occurred within Old Order society, but attempts have been made to carefully control the magnitude, rate and direction of change.

CHAPTER THREE: METHODS

Introduction

The current study is a descriptive, agricultural case study based on fieldwork carried out during the months of February through June and October, 1989, in the Old Order Amish community in Buchanan County, Iowa. The theoretical frameworks of ethnoscience, cognitive anthropology and farmer-centered research provided the foundation for the study. The goal of the study is to describe the essential components of the Amish farming system, and to uncover emic views of phenomena, beliefs and behavior that support the system.

To use this approach effectively, the cultural context must be understood from the perspective of its members. Agricultural practices must not be isolated from the cultural context; the beliefs and values that created and now maintain the current traditions must be explored. Often, farming practices have been misunderstood, and farmers viewed as ignorant, because no one took the time to understand why farmers were doing what they were doing. Underlying values (cultural and personal) always provide a meaningful explanation for peoples' decisions and practices. The cultural context of the farming system must, therefore, be understood before one can determine how knowledge from this system might be useful in addressing current issues facing the larger agricultural community.

The specific objectives of the study are to (1) describe contemporary Amish farming knowledge and practices in Iowa; (2) identify the decision-making processes and goals used to guide change within the system; (3) outline the values which support agricultural decisions and practices; and (4) explore the possible connections between social structure and agricultural practices.

Amish agriculture is so intertwined with the whole of Amish culture and society that arbitrarily isolating this aspect of Amish society may result in some knowledge about agriculture, but with little understanding about how this fits into the overall picture. Amish culture is often confusing to outsiders because the connections are not easily apparent. For example, one Amish man explains, "our simple living is not an end in itself, but a means of strengthening family, church and community bonds" (Stoll and Stoll 1980, 13). The reasons behind farming decisions and practices must be examined in this context.

Definitions

Several key definitions have provided the conceptual foundation for the study. These terms will be outlined to identify the basic assumptions of the researcher and place the study in its proper context. "Every human being presupposes and assumes, comprehends reality in terms of learned concepts and relationships, and continuously categorizes and catalogues phenomena intellectually" (Georges and Jones 1980, 41-42). This does not rule out objectivity, but recognizes that human beings, with their accompanying assumptions, are central in this type of research.

The farming system

The basic unit of analysis used in the study is the family-operated farm. The farms in this study cannot be understood by isolating and analyzing one variable such as soil type or yield per acre, although these variables also need to be studied. They are part of a larger whole, or farming system, and must be examined in this context. A farming system, according to Shaner et al. (1982, 3),

> is the complex arrangement of soils, water sources, crops, livestock, labor, and other resources and characteristics within an environmental setting that the farm family manages in accordance with its preferences, capabilities, and available technologies.

In other words, the farming system includes internal and external factors (such as family labor availability and market prices), as well as tangible and intangible inputs (such as natural resources and family goals and values). A farming system is a complex set of interrelated factors, and these individual components need to be examined in relationship to one another. This study does not attempt to examine every possible factor and its connections to every other factor, but it does seek to present a view which represents the wholeness and interconnectedness involved on the Amish family farm.

This approach is necessary if research is to be of practical value or have meaning for its participants. As Rhoades (1984, 41) suggests, "compartmentalized research in agriculture often leads to laboratory or experiment station scientists who have little knowledge about farming." A person may be an expert on reproduction in sheep, for example, but not understand how this is important to or affects farmers on a daily basis.

Ethnoscience

According to Sturtevant (1964, 99 and 100), ethno "refers to the system of knowledge and cognition typical of a given culture" and ethnoscience is a given culture's particular way of "classifying its material and social culture." The goal of ethnoscience is to discover and describe a culture's classification system in its own terms, from its own perspective.

The importance of understanding the cultural context cannot be overstated. The ethnoscientist cannot simply list the phenomena or behavior which is observed; the ethnoscientist must discover and interpret meaningful phenomena and the principles which give meaning to those phenomena. As Charles Frake (1980, 2) suggests, "In actuality not even the most concrete, objectively apparent physical object can be identified apart from some culturally defined system of concepts." In other words, ethnoscientific efforts must reflect the cultural context which gives meaning to the phenomena under investigation. "Culture provides principles for framing experience as eventful in particular ways..." (Frake 1980, 58). Without this context, information simply becomes a dead artifact, separated from any practical meaning and, therefore, essentially useless.

Culture

Culture is a word as diverse in meaning as the realities it describes. Thus, it has been defined in a variety of ways. In this study, culture is understood as "the acquired knowledge that people use to interpret experience and generate social behavior" (Spradley 1979, 5). Culture provides a "set of standards" people use to operate within their society (Goodenough 1981, 55). Spradley (1979) equates culture with a "cognitive map", but Frake (1980, 58) says "culture does not provide a cognitive map, but rather a set of principles for map-making and navigation." A culture provides a set of guiding principles people use to determine appropriate behavior and make decisions.

Cognitive anthropology

Given these definitions of culture, cognitive anthropologists seek to discover and understand the way people conceptualize phenomena, structure reality and make decisions. In order to make these discoveries, cognitive anthropologists observe how people talk about phenomena. "Culturally significant cognitive features must be communicable between persons in one of the standard symbolic systems of the culture" (Frake 1980, 3). Usually this occurs through language. But, "language is only one form of communication, the most obvious" (Powdermaker 1966, 289). Non-verbal behavior is also important. Often, for example, what people say and what they do are two different things. Language alone does not paint the complete picture, and, therefore, language along with its accompanying behavior must be examined.

Cultural relevance

"If we want to account for behavior by relating it to the conditions under which it normally occurs, we require procedures for discovering what people are attending to, what information they are processing, when they reach decisions which lead to culturally appropriate behavior" (Frake 1964, 133). In this same article, Frake points out that the anthropologist seeks to discover the set of rules for culturally appropriate behavior rather than predicting or prescribing such behavior.

The process leading to these discoveries must itself be based on culturally appropriate methods. "Since the ethnoscientific method aims at discovering culturally relevant discriminations and categorizations, it is essential that the discovery procedures themselves be relevant to the culture under investigation" (Sturtevant 1964, 111). Without culturally relevant procedures, observations and outcomes will be useless. "Methods link data -- what we construe to be observations of some particular reality -- with theory, our proposals for understanding reality in general" (Frake 1980, 46). Appropriate links between methods, observations and theory are therefore crucial.

Frake (1964, 132) suggests that "both the queries and their reponses are to be discovered in the culture of the people being studied." This process will take time, but it is absolutely essential because without it, the principles "discovered" by the researcher are likely to be imposed from an outside and alien perspective. This imposition will result in studies of little practical value, either to the larger society or to participants. It will also contribute to the inappropriate labeling of phenomena. For example, traditional agriculture and alternative agriculture in the United States have often been viewed as backward, unscientific and primitive (Otto and Burns 1981; Altieri 1983). This is most unfortunate because traditional agriculture is a rich source of accumulated cultural wisdom. But because of the way such agriculture has been labeled, its value has often been overlooked.

Farmer-centered research

The preceding definitions lead naturally to an orientation which places farmers at the center of the agricultural research process. Even if farmers do not participate directly (though direct participation is crucial), an effort must be made to see things from the farmers' perspectives. This can only be accomplished when researchers have a "basic respect for farmers, their knowledge and their competence" (Chambers 1988, 11).

One way to learn how and what farmers think is to have "direct, sustained contact with the people studied in their everyday lives and on their terms" (Rhoades 1984, 40). This can be accomplished by working with participant farmers (Howes and Chambers 1980; Rhoades 1984), but, whatever the specific methods, it requires that outsiders listen and learn from farmers (Chambers 1988).

Indigenous knowledge systems

An indigenous knowledge system encompasses knowledge itself and the various means and processes by which knowledge is used or transformed within the system (Howes and Chambers 1980). Indigenous knowledge is cultural knowledge -- specific to a given group within a society. It "represents successful ways in which people have dealt with their environment" (Warren 1989, 5). Indigenous knowledge reflects the unique experience, values, preferences and perceptions which guide daily activities and decision making. It is a dynamic source of creativity and innovation.

Although there is no doubt that farmers experiment (Rhoades 1987, 1984; Chambers 1988; Altieri 1983; Richards 1985), little is known about the methods they use. Farmer experimentation has, more often than not, been overlooked by agricultural researchers because it has not been recognized as legitimate or scientific. Rhoades (1987, 15) asserts that

> the similarities with the scientific method are clear. The difference, however, is that farmers have very specific goals in mind and the results of experimentation must be practical. There is no room for experimentation strictly for the sake of experimentation.

Based on their experience and experimentation, farmers make generalizations that can be applied to specific circumstances. This knowledge of farmers is a resource which must be respected if research is to be of any practical value.

Framework

The epistemological framework for this approach has been provided through the Center for Indigenous Knowledge for Agriculture and Rural Development, CIKARD, at Iowa State University. CIKARD acts as a clearinghouse for collecting, documenting, and disseminating information on indigenous agricultural knowledge; develops methodologies for recording indigenous knowledge systems; conducts training courses on indigenous knowledge; and facilitates interdisciplinary research on indigenous knowledge (CIKARD 1988).

Four underlying assumptions about indigenous knowledge provide a basis for this study's approach. First, indigenous knowledge is practical knowledge. Second, indigenous knowledge reflects generations of experience (Warren 1989; Berry 1977). Third, indigenous knowledge is dynamic, innovative, flexible and adaptive. And, fourth, there are lessons to be learned from indigenous knowledge that can be applied to other situations.

The practicality of indigenous knowledge has two sides. It is practical because it works for the people who use it, and because it can also benefit those outside the system who learn from it. Learning about indigenous knowledge facilitates two-way communication and has the potential to inform research priorities. Research will be more relevant and of more direct benefit to farmers if it reflects their reality, concerns and knowledge. One must ask, "What are the practical implications from traditional wisdom that can be applied to current concerns?"

The framework also assumes indigenous knowledge is based on accumulated experience (Warren 1989). As Berry (1977, 45) suggests, "A good farmer...is a cultural product; he is made by a sort of training, certainly, in what his time imposes or demands, but he is also made by generations of experience."

While indigenous knowledge is specific knowledge, it is also dynamic and flexible. Farmer innovations and adaptations modify the knowledge system over time as farmers respond to the changing demands of their physical and social environments. Therefore, "indigenous knowledge is dynamic; it changes through indigenous creativity and innovativeness as well as through contact with other knowledge systems" (Warren 1989, 5). Farmers in all parts of the world actively experiment with new ideas and practices, but little attention is paid to this fact, with even less known about how they go about it (Rhoades 1987; Richards 1985).

Indigenous knowledge works for farmers in specific situations, but also has the potential to be applied to address problems in other circumstances. For example, a potato storage technique (used by farmers) involving diffused light was observed in several parts of the world and subsequently was able to be adapted by other farmers in different environments (Rhoades 1987).

Indigenous knowledge is cultural knowledge -- knowledge which is specific and yet dynamic, knowledge which has been adapted to the physical and social environment in which it is used. Indigenous knowledge is practical knowledge because it is the knowledge which guides life on a daily basis. Indigenous knowledge represents a source of ideas and adaptations whose implications can be explored and applied to address problems in other settings. All of these qualities, however, cannot be realized unless one understands the system in its own terms. That is the goal of the present study.

Procedures

The study was carried out using participant-observation, informal discussions and formal interviews. (1) This approach was chosen because it has been found to be the most effective and the least objectionable to participants (Loomis 1979; Olshan 1980; Huntington 1956). Pre-prepared formal questionnaires will uncover some information, but given the status of higher education and pride within Old Order society, these efforts are likely to be met with qualified resignation (Savells and Foster 1987). Within Amish society, "the ideal person remains quietly in the background" (Ericksen and Klein 1981, 294). Olshan (1980, 60-61) contends that the Amish are deferential to interviewers because they believe the interviewer "is likely to feel superior. The Amishman is likely to play along with this imputed status differential in order to expedite the completion of the interview. The emphasis he places on submission actually prescribes this response. Consequently he will be content to let the outsider leave with accurate answers to irrelevant questions."

Ideally, we would like to hear about Amish agriculture directly from Amish people themselves. If possible, I would prefer to let the Amish tell their own story. But the Amish do not desire attention and are reluctant to explain their ways in a public setting. As a result, observations by an outsider must often be the primary vehicle for understanding the Amish.

Observations of this kind are necessary and may provide helpful information and insight. But it must be remembered that the person making the analysis is not the real expert. No outsider -- in any situation -- can completely and accurately comprehend the intricate workings of the group they observe and to which they do not belong. Conclusions, therefore, must be presented honestly and humbly, without the pretense of providing a complete and definitive analysis. An outsider's observations represent only one piece of the puzzle.

It must also be remembered that any individual member of a group does not possess the complete picture either. Each member of a group has knowledge unique to his or her individual position. But each member of a group also has knowledge that is group knowledge, that is, knowledge common to any member of the group. Huntington (1956, 1038) believes that in an Old Order Amish community "knowledge and beliefs are shared to a greater extent than is the case in most communities in this country. There is a large area of overlap between what one Amishman knows and believes and what all Amishmen know and believe." These different kinds of knowledge must be kept in mind as the results of the study are presented. Each observer, both inside and outside the group, has potentially valuable contributions to make to the construction of an overall picture.

The Amish settlement in Buchanan County was chosen as the study site because it is the second-largest and second-oldest Amish community in Iowa, and because little previous research has been done in this community. It was also selected because it offered the opportunity to start from scratch in the fieldwork process. The Kalona community is the largest and oldest Amish community in Iowa, but it is also fairly well-known to Iowans and the researcher had had previous experience in the community. The Buchanan County site was conveniently located, represented a new experience for the researcher and was an area which had not been previously explored.

The initial contact in the community was established through a previous family acquaintance in the Kalona area. During the first three months, regular visits were made to the community. A primary contact was established during this time and many additional contacts were made through personal visits recommended by the initial participants.

After initially visiting the community on a regular basis for three months, two months were then spent living with and working for several families in the community. Primary contact was maintained with six households. In total, between twenty and twenty-five households participated in the study. Although the opportunity to live with Amish families provided immediate access to the community, it also limited interaction because of the role women play in Amish society. Men and women work together within the family, but in public settings men and women have very limited contact. Men and women also do different kinds of work on the farm. Men and women are both involved in doing the daily chores, such as milking the cows; women, however, typically do not do much fieldwork unless there is a shortage of labor, such as few children or few sons within the family (Ericksen and Klein 1981; Participants 14 and 20).

As a young, educated, female researcher, my range of interaction was limited. My primary duties were associated with the operation of the household and in this position I was not able to have as much contact with the male members of the community who carry out the majority of the farming activities, such as fieldwork. However, a level of mutual trust, respect and acceptance was established which allowed considerable flexibility, and household observations and informal conversations provided essential information about the farming system. My background as a Mennonite also provided an outlook on life and sensitivity to Amish culture which proved useful.

A major component of the study was time. Time was spent listening and observing so the researcher could learn to ask the right questions. Some initial questions were prepared based on the hypothesis about the stability of the Amish farming system, but the majority were asked after the researcher had spent time in the community. This was done to avoid, as much as possible, the imposition of preconceived ideas. For example, yield per unit of land is typically used as the primary, and often the sole, indicator of success when a conventional American farmer's operation is being evaluated. In the Amish system, making this assumption would have been misleading and would have distorted the findings because it ignores the complex interactions within the total farming system -- interactions that occur between the various crops grown, in crop/animal relationships and in the socio-religious/agricultural relationship. Furthermore, this assumption is based on the faulty idea that yield per unit of land is the most valued measure of success for the Amish (Olshan 1980; Jackson 1984). Instead of being based on external assumptions, the questions must arise out of the cultural context -- the social, economic, physical and phenomenological matrix.

Relevant literature from other Amish community studies was reviewed in preparation for the fieldwork, and is used throughout the discussion to highlight various points. The details of a comparison from another community may differ, but the underlying characteristics are similar. Just as each Amish individual varies in his or her degree of adherence to the Amish ideal, so too each community, and even each church district, translates the Amish ideal into slightly different realities (Stoltzfus 1977). The general principles are assumed to be similar, even though there are slight variations among communities, because those who do not conform closely enough to the ideal will be forced to sever ties with the church or will remove themselves.

Presentation of Data

Given the qualitative, non-technical nature of this report, the data "appear in words rather than in numbers" (Miles and Huberman 1984, 20). A primary reason for this approach is the interconnected nature of the Amish farming system and Amish society. There is a place for studies which focus on and quantify one or a limited number of specific variables within the system; the goal of this study, however, is to make explicit the complex and dynamic nature of Amish agriculture, and its place within the larger Amish culture.

The title of the report, "Amish Agriculture in Iowa: A Preliminary Investigation," refers to the exploratory nature of this case study. The goal of an exploratory case study is "to develop ideas for further study" (Yin 1984, 10). In this type of process, conclusions provide the basis for generating new hypotheses. This study attempts to provide the background needed to stimulate further investigation. As Georges and Jones (1980, 152) point out,

> The results of fieldwork, therefore, are not ends. What is learned from the experience results instead in continuities and new beginnings whose ends are usually unpredictable and indeterminable. Such is the nature of human relationships and of human beings' constant search to understand themselves and know each other.

It is hoped that what has been learned from this process will contribute to the generation of additional questions, as well as provide some insight into current questions.

In the following chapter, the four objectives of (1) describing contemporary Amish farming knowledge and practices in Iowa; (2) identifying the decision-making processes and goals used to guide change within the system; (3) outlining the values which support agricultural decisions and practices; and (4) exploring the possible connections between social structure and agricultural practices, will serve as the main topical divisions. Each major section will begin with a short story, based on the fieldwork, to illustrate the findings. A discussion of the findings will follow each story.

Summary

The techniques used in the study were chosen to provide a balance between a scientific method often seen as cold and impersonal, and a research process that reflects the humanness of the researcher and the participants (see Agar 1980). The assumptions have been outlined to make the reader aware of the biases which exist and have influenced the course of the study. As Werner and Schoepfle (1987, 171) point out, "not all biases are bad, but one must strive to make one's biases explicit... ." This chapter has made these biases clear.

Although the topic lends itself to a general exposition, four areas have been chosen for specific analysis. It is hoped that these areas will serve to illustrate the characteristics of the Amish farming system and that they will provide impetus for further study. Ideas generated by the investigation will be discussed in the concluding chapter.

The Amish farming system provides an example which appears anachronistic, but which has the potential to speak to issues which are of current critical importance. A model built on the past is now relevant to our present and future circumstances.

Note

1. In order to preserve a measure of anonymity, all individuals cited as references have been assigned a participant number. A brief description of each participant is given in the section following the bibliography entitled "List of Participants."

CHAPTER FOUR: FINDINGS AND DISCUSSION

Introduction

The ideal and most prestigious occupation for the Old Order Amish is farming. In the oldest and largest Amish communities, however, deriving one's income solely from farming is becoming more difficult to accomplish. Meyers (1983b) estimates that in many of these large communities, less than half of the Amish household heads are farmers. "With continuing growth in their population and a dwindling supply of land there is little hope for the coming generations to be primarily farmers" (179).

Several strategies have been devised to deal with the declining opportunities in agriculture. One response has been to continually shop for land where new communities can be formed (Luthy 1985; Yoder 1989). New businesses have also been established (Kraybill 1989; Participants 1, 2 and 15). Although many businesses are run in conjunction with the farm, others are operated by Amish men who do not farm. Amish women also operate home-based businesses. Some businesses, such as harness and buggy shops, cater primarily to Amish needs within the community. Other businesses, such as furniture making and general carpentry, satisfy needs within the Amish community and also for non-Amish customers. A few businesses, bakeries and quilt shops for example, depend primarily on non-Amish customers. Locally-run, rural-based businesses keep money in the community and enable a family to continue farming or at least to remain in the community if they do not farm. On-farm businesses also keep the family together, a high priority among the Amish. Daily, wage labor outside the community, in factories for example, is the least desirable employment option and was once prohibited in many communities. Those who must take such employment do it with the hope of eventually being able to buy their own farms (Meyers 1983b; Participant 8).

In Iowa, the majority of household heads still derive their primary source of income from farming. But the number of small, on-farm businesses continues to increase and more Amish men now depend on some form of wage labor than they did twenty years ago (Participant 2). In the 1980s a new community was started where land was more readily available and cheaper than in several of the older communities. As the Amish settle in an area, and as the community grows, the demand for farmland rises and the value also increases. This naturally leads to land shortages. Land shortages encourage land shopping in other areas, and the need for additional income, like that which a small business can provide. When couples marry and want to begin farming, they first must usually work for an established farmer (Amish or non-Amish), rent available farms and then purchase their own place. This means couples usually move a number of times before they are able to establish themselves on their own farm. The fortunate few are able to settle immediately on a farm purchased with their parents' backing or on the "home place." Because the Amish have large families, it is difficult to provide a farm for every child. This is one reason the demand for land is always strong in an Amish community (Yoder 1989).

Despite the increasing number of non-farming Amish, the Amish as a whole remain an agricultural people. Nearly every Amish couple hopes to farm, and farming remains the occupation of choice. In the following sections, entitled Practice, Predicaments, Philosophy and Cultural

Patterns, the central aspects of the Amish farming system will be discussed. The four sections will be subdivided into two components, introduction and discussion. Each introduction section will focus on the story of David and Alma Martin - a fictitious Amish family. In several places, quotes from sources written by real Amish people will be used to describe what David or Alma might think or say.

Practice

<u>Introduction</u>

The summer had been a good one. The final harvest was just around the corner, and Alma Martin (1) was sure it would be an adequate reward for their efforts. The Martins' 80-acre farm produced the basic necessities for their family and farm animals and was always alive with activity. But even with the constant activity, the farm was a quiet, peaceful place, where the laughter of children and the squeak of the windmill could easily be heard. As members of the more traditional Old Order Amish, the Martins owned no tractors or power equipment, their farmwork accomplished with horse power and small gasoline or diesel engines. In the house, no noise from a refrigerator, furnace or air conditioner and no telephone, radio or television interrupted the daily routine.

Throughout the summer, Alma had tended their large garden and had canned countless jars of fruits and vegetables. Every morning (and evening) she, along with her husband David and their two oldest sons, ages 12 and 13, would milk the family's sixteen dairy cows before the creamery truck picked up the milk at 7 a. m. Milk was their primary source of cash income, with the sale of soybeans and feeder pigs providing some additional money. In the past, every Amish family owned their own chickens and sold eggs, but now only a few families kept chickens because there was no longer a market for eggs. Even without the chickens, the Martins' farm was a diversified operation.

The Martins' 80 acres was a stark contrast to the quarter-section of conventionally-farmed land bordering them to the west and owned by an absentee landlord. On the conventionally-farmed acres there were no fences, no trees and no buildings. The only crops grown on this land were corn and soybeans. After a heavy rain, evidence of erosion was apparent from the rivers of soil which ended up in the roadside ditches.

The Martins' farm, on the other hand, consisted of six small, fenced fields (the largest being fifteen acres and the smallest, eleven acres) and a farmstead with two houses, a large barn, a granary and several small sheds. There were trees on the building site and an occasional tree in a fencerow. The fields were fenced to accommodate livestock and were cropped according to several variations of a five-year cycle: one year of corn, one year of soybeans, one year of oats and two years of an alfalfa, clover and grass mixture -- the first year harvested for hay and the second year pastured; or, two years of corn, one year of oats and two years of the alfalfa, clover and grass mixture. The rotations eliminated the need for insecticides and limited the amount of herbicides which could be applied due to carryover concerns. Manure from the livestock was supplemented with small amounts of commercial fertilizers. David Martin estimated that his commercial fertilizer applications were about one-fourth that of his non-Amish neighbor.

David owned eight strong work horses whose use he believed helped minimize soil compaction, and in turn, weeds. When asked about his farming practices David might have had this to say:

> We do all our field work with horses. We farm eighty acres, growing feed for our dairy herd. We plow the soil in the fall with six horses and a two-bottom plow. In the spring, we cut up the soil with a disk, and level it and work it with a spring-tooth harrow. We use a drill to sow anywhere from 12 to 20 acres of oats, which we cut at harvest time with a grain binder and three horses. ... We also plant 12 to 15 acres of corn, with which to fill our two silos. The corn is cut with a corn binder pulled by three horses. It is hauled to the silos on wagons and handfed into an ensilage chopper. ... Our horses are also used for many other jobs, from cutting, raking, and loading hay to hauling manure (Stoll and Stoll 1980, 25).

Although the Martin farm was small and depended on the use of technology considered outdated and backward by conventional farmers, David and Alma knew this was the best way to maintain the way of life which their faith required.

Discussion: Inputs

Labor. In the most traditional Old Order settlements, human labor (supplied by the family) and animal traction make up the largest share of the total labor input. An Amish farm is management and labor intensive. Labor is substituted for capital, resulting in the need for the whole family and, at times, other helpers such as neighbors and relatives to participate in the farm operation. Routine tasks which require extra labor, such as making hay and threshing oats, are done with extended family members or Amish neighbors. Special projects, such as building a new hog shed, are accomplished by announcing a "frolic." A frolic is a day when friends, neighbors and relatives work together to help the family with the special need. Frolics are routine, not rare, occurrences among the Amish. Labor is also supplied by community members when illness or natural disaster cause an unusual need.

According to Craumer's (1977) observations, mechanization on Amish farms would reduce the demand for labor (displace people) and could lead to larger and, therefore, fewer farms. The Amish community depends on the presence and close proximity of many Amish farm families, and larger and fewer farms would destroy this pattern. Labor also makes use of the entire family, which is a way for parents to control the socialization of their children, and which strengthens the family as an institution in the Amish community. This is an example of how the social structure of the Amish community affects agricultural practices.

Energy. Energy inputs on a traditional Amish farm are primarily from renewable sources. Wind power is used to pump water, human energy is used to milk cows and pick corn, horses are used for fieldwork and animal waste is used for fertilizer. Non-renewable energy is used in the form of fuel, commercial fertilizers and pesticides. Contrary to popular belief, the Amish are not organic farmers. There are Amish farmers who farm organically, that is, without the use of commercial fertilizers or pesticides, but the majority of Amish farmers use some commercial fertilizer and/or pesticides. The use of commercial fertilizers and pesticides among the Amish has grown in the past twenty years (Participants 4 and 8; Erb 1987).

Capital. Although the Amish farming system is labor intensive rather than capital intensive, capital investment is certainly needed in the Amish operation. Horse-drawn machinery, tools, horses, land and buildings are all examples of capital requirements for the Amish farmer. According to one study, the level of technology used by the Amish has helped them "avoid the major causes of small farm poverty and bankruptcy, the difficulty of obtaining the capital to purchase modern agricultural machinery or the heavy debt payments required if it is obtained" (Johnson et al. 1977, 375). The Amish have evidently learned to use the level of technology appropriate to maintain the scale of farming they prefer.

Knowledge. Many agricultural practices of the Amish are based on generations of experience. The Amish have been farming for several centuries in the United States and prior to that in Europe; farming is part of their identity and has taken on spiritual significance (Schwieder 1973; Hostetler 1980a). Farms, and the knowledge and values needed to maintain them, have been passed down through the generations. Old people are respected in Amish society. In the family, parents teach their children what is expected of them. The Amish prefer practical education, learning to farm by working on the farm, for example. Amish children go to school through the eighth grade, usually in one-room country schools which are operated by the Amish themselves. They believe "that if a child is to remain a farmer, he has no need of the elaborate and useless education provided by the high school; it is better for him to work on the farm and acquire a practical knowledge of husbandry" (Thoreau 1980, 115). For the most part, the Amish depend on their own knowledge systems -- to repair machinery and to treat animal health problems, for example (Participants 8 and 9). Ideas and innovations which work for one Amish farmer will quickly circulate through informal conversational channels, which are the main transmitters of information and news within an Amish community and among communities.

Management. The farm management system of the Old Order Amish is complex. Amish farmers own their own farms and make many decisions on their own, but their decisions are not individualistic and their farms are not totally independent operations. Amish farmers are not out there "on their own." They typically have extended family members in the community, have probably borrowed money from within the community or loaned money to other Amish farmers, receive help from and give help to neighbors and relatives and know that in the event of an emergency, such as illness or fire, the Amish community will provide assistance. The community, at the church district level, also determines the basic standards which the Amish farmer must follow. These standards typically pertain to type, size and use of farm machinery, mode of dairy operation (whether to milk by hand or with machines, for example) and the way in which various types of engines can be used. These standards are agreed upon by the members of the congregation or the community as a whole if there are only a few congregations.

The Amish farm cannot be understood if it is examined as an independent unit. The Amish farm is not an isolated entity; its vitality flows from its place within the Amish community. As Logsdon (1988, 30) argues, Amish society "sanctifies for the individual the virtues that make good farming or good work of any kind possible: a prudent practice of ecology, moderation, simplicity of life, frugality, interdependence (neighborliness), family stability, and financial common sense -- the traditional rural American values that mainstream culture appears to be abandoning." And it does this within the context of "a supportive, tight-knit community." The Amish farmer, therefore, is not alone. Management skills do vary from person to person (some Amish farmers are better managers than others), but all Amish farmers can depend on the community to which they belong and the values which are constantly reinforced there.

Predicaments

<u>Introduction</u>

    With the harvest nearing completion, Alma's thoughts turned toward the upcoming council church and communion. This was the time of year when the church reviewed its standards and asked its members to evaluate their relationships with each other and to confirm their agreement with the church's teachings. This year Alma was worried about her youngest sister. Since spring communion, Miriam's husband had begun to use an engine run by compressed air in his machine shop, a convenience forbidden by their church. The issue had not been addressed directly during the summer, but with communion coming up it was sure to be examined. Alma knew that these discussions would be an emotional time for the church. All of the church members knew a certain amount of change was inevitable; they could see this by looking at the differences between their own childhood and their children's circumstances. But change was never accepted immediately or automatically. A period of prolonged evaluation was necessary before the use of a new innovation could be accepted. And even then, some innovations, such as milking machines, had never been accepted in Alma's community.

    Alma's father-in-law was a bishop in Alma's church district. When he had been ordained to this office, he had promised to keep a tight rein on change. Given this task, the bishop had to be the proper example and enforce the regulations the church had agreed upon. Alma knew this was not an easy job.

    Alma knew too that proposed changes always affected more than one individual. One change could easily lead to another. A minister had once explained that "we try to find out how new ideas, inventions or trends will affect us as people, as a community, as a church. If they affect us adversely, we are wary. Many things are not what they appear to be at first glance. It is not the individual links that concern us, but the total chain. Often one thing leads to another" (Stoll and Stoll 1980, 16). Alma's people did not believe technology was evil in itself, but they were concerned with how its use would influence the family, church and community as a whole. Given their position as a semi-isolated, rural, religious community, they wanted to moderate the influences of change from the outside world.

    In Alma's community, tractors and large, modern machinery were forbidden because such expensive, labor-saving technology would eventually upset the balance of the community. If farmers had to go into debt to purchase such equipment, they would need more land to support the payments. More land could only be gained by putting a neighbor out of business. If Amish neighbors were forced out of farming, the community would be destroyed. Reducing the demand for labor would also mean a farmer's children would no longer be needed on the farm. They would be forced to seek other employment, which would weaken family bonds and expose the children to unwanted, external influences. A small change in farm equipment would thus have a major impact on the structure of the farm itself, threatening the family and the community. Alma and her husband could not think of themselves alone when they considered using a new innovation.

Discussion: Continuity and change

The goals and decision-making processes which an Amish farm family use to guide daily life operate primarily at the church district level. According to Huntington (1956, 1046), "it is within the congregation that all important decisions are made." Members of a church district understand what is expected of them. Individual farmers in the same district do not do everything exactly alike, but the basic characteristics of their operations will be similar. For example, they will use the same level of technology, all milking by hand and farming with horses if these are the standards followed in their particular congregation.

As pointed out earlier, new technology is not assumed to be desirable just because it is new. "Technological advances and economic growth are increasingly questioned rather than being unthinkingly treated as synonymous with progress" (Olshan 1980, 167). The Amish are aware that in their community, too much progress too quickly has the potential to disrupt the balance of the society. Therefore, changes in technology are carefully regulated within the church.

Change occurs slowly in an Amish community. Changes that are eventually accepted, usually long after the technology was new to the broader society, are negotiated through an informal and gradual process. The accepted changes may not be officially recognized for a generation or more, and typically are not sanctioned by the church even after they have been widely used. The process of change often begins with illicit use of a restricted innovation, usually by a single individual or family. These initial attempts at change are often thwarted by the church, but often they begin again and gradually are tolerated implicitly even while they are still officially restricted. This process will eventually lead to widespread use of the change; informal, tacit acceptance; and after sufficient time has passed, to a more formal acceptance.

Faith, farm and family, the three essential elements suggested by Hostetler (1951), are central in Amish life, and the goals in one area also affect decisions in the other two areas. The Amish recognize that the ability to maintain their culture depends on the interaction of many factors and the willingness to examine the connections between various decisions. Cultural strength can only be achieved by maintaining the integrity of each contributing element. The vitality of the small farm depends on the strength of the family, and the strength of the church depends on the endurance of the family and the farm. As LeCompte (1984, 16) has maintained, "to understand Amish agriculture, one must understand the spiritual and social context in which the Amish live. Family and community unity and Christian faith are wholly integrated into Amish life such that they cannot be isolated as separate aspects... ." Faith, farm and family bind the system together.

Potential changes are evaluated in this context. For example, the compressed air engine is not the central concern of Alma's community, but rather the effects the introduction of such a change will have on the total system. When an Amish farmer in Ohio wrote about his objection to the introduction of no-till farming methods in the Amish community (supported by the county extension service and chemical companies), he described how no-till farming would affect his relationship with his neighbor:

> With no-till I would have the means to farm his 50 tillable acres, in addition to my own, and he could be 'free' to work off the farm. I know I wouldn't be able to do the excellent farming he is doing now, and I would miss the rich fragrance of his fertile soil. And more than that, I would miss my neighbor (Kline 1986, 10).

Outsiders who are unfamiliar with these realities will not recognize the soundness of the Amish decision to reject certain innovations. Misperceptions of Amish agriculture lead to statements such as "other than the fact that they farm with horses, Amish farmers are no different than other farmers" (Participant 19). These kinds of simplistic attitudes prevent the success of Amish agriculture from being comprehended.

Even though it has been frequently predicted that the Old Order Amish will, sooner or later, assimilate with mainstream culture and lose their distinctive identity, Amish culture remains strong and somewhat separate from the broader society. While the Amish have been forced to make some concessions to the dominant culture, they have successfully negotiated their place within that culture. They choose what is useful and reject what would weaken their way of life.

Philosophy

Introduction

As she packed lunches for her five school-age children, Alma thought ahead to the tasks of the day. David could hardly wait to begin preparing the fields for sowing oats, but the late-March soil was still too wet. With the horses, David could often begin working the soil before tractors could get into the field, but David was careful not to start too early in the season because a person could ruin the soil structure if the fields were too wet. He was always eager to find ways to reduce soil compaction because weeds seemed to thrive in compacted soil. He also believed in promoting an environment favorable for earthworms.

Today David was going to help an Amish family on the other side of the settlement who had lost their granary in a windstorm. While David was gone, Alma would go to help her neighbor, Mrs. Miller, get ready for church. This Sunday was the Millers' turn to host the biweekly church service. Preparing for church was a big task, so Alma and Mrs. Miller helped each other when it was their turns. The three youngest children who were not in school would also go along. Sometimes the three-year-old twins stayed with Alma's parents, who lived in the dody (grandpa) house, but today they would go and play with the Miller children.

On Sunday the twenty-five families in the southwest district would gather at the Miller farm for the traditional three-hour service. The families knew each other well because they lived in the same area of the settlement, worked together and were accountable to each other. In addition, they shared a similar identity: they all spoke the same language, wore the same style of clothes, lived on small farms or small acreages, embraced the same faith and practiced the same plain lifestyle which distinguished them from their non-Amish neighbors. No one in Alma and David's congregation could remain anonymous; membership required face-to-face relationships. Just last month David had explained to their non-Amish cousin, visiting from another state, that "being Amish to me is belonging and being needed in the community, neighborhood, family and church" (Larimore and Taylor 1985). The closeness of the small congregation was something David, Alma and their children took for granted. Anything else would have seemed strange.

Discussion: Values and agriculture

Members of Amish society possess basic assumptions which often run counter to those common in mainstream American culture. This makes it difficult for the average American to understand Amish culture. In the Amish farming system, specific practices are followed because of certain underlying principles and values. The practices of conventional farmers also reflect a certain value orientation. Values will always be behind the choice of agricultural practices. Aldo Leopold recognized this and proposed that a land ethic must precede changes in farming methods (Leopold 1984). Unfortunately, very little is said about this in current models of adoption and change. This deficiency must be addressed so that alternatives to conventional agriculture can be adopted and maintained.

Conformity. In Amish society, members must conform to the standards the church requires. Dressing alike (in styles now obsolete in mainstream society), speaking Pennsylvania German as their first and primary language, using horses on the farm, attending their own schools and restricting the use of certain conveniences are all symbols of separateness from the dominant American culture and mechanisms that create a strong group consciousness. An Amish person belongs to a group and their primary identity is as a group member rather than as an individual. "When we're baptized into the church we lose our individuality, we join one body" (Larimore and Taylor 1985).

The importance of being together, in work and in play, is imparted to children from the time they are born. An Amish child is typically born into a large family, and contact with grandparents, aunts, uncles, cousins, neighbors and friends is frequent. In one family, a mother expressed concern for a young child who was playing alone because she did not want the child to think she could have everything for herself (Yoder 1989). The focus is always on one's place in the group and not on one's individuality.

The expression of togetherness and conformity in Amish society affects agriculture in several ways. First, it means an Amish farmer has a strong support network and can depend on receiving financial and other forms of assistance. This is demonstrated within the family and within the community as a whole. On the farm, the whole family works together and in the community few activities of any kind are done alone. Second, Amish farmers are expected to farm in ways beneficial for the whole Amish community. They must have labor and money to share, and must treat the land well because it is to be passed on to future generations of Amish farmers.

Cooperation. The togetherness present in Amish society is a close cousin to cooperation. In order to work together successfully, all participants must cooperate. Although competition is evident in Amish society, cooperation is the stronger force. The well-known barn raisings, where the whole community helps to erect a new barn in the place of one destroyed by fire or other natural disaster, is the most obvious case of cooperation and mutual assistance. But Amish families assist each other with routine tasks too. Neighbors and relatives (neighbors are often relatives) work together to make hay, thresh oats, build new buildings, quilt, care for the sick and to prepare for weddings, funerals and regular church services. The Amish community also operates as an insurance policy for its members. Instead of relying on insurance companies for protection, the Amish practice mutual aid. For example, when a family cannot pay a large hospital bill, the community comes to their aid. All families in the church are asked to contribute money according to their own ability, and the donations are then used to pay the bill. The Amish do not accept government assistance such as social security and they do not participate in agricultural programs such as crop set-aside programs. Whatever assistance they need is provided from within the Amish community.

These examples show that cooperation is strong in Amish society, but the practice of cooperation has also changed over the years. One person indicated that twenty years ago the Amish worked together and with their non-Amish neighbors even more than they do now. For example, non-Amish farmers used to be part of threshing rings. Now they no longer participate, primarily because they have discarded the methods the Amish have retained, and because they no longer need to depend on this form of mutual assistance (Participant 13). Another source indicated that competition appears to be stronger among the Amish than it used to be. For example, everyone wants to be first to finish picking their corn in the fall, so everyone tries to hurry as much as possible (Participant 11). Changes in cooperation are also reflected in changing patterns of ownership. It is now common for each farmer to own nearly all of the major pieces of farm equipment needed for the farm operation. This means that there is less dependence on other Amish farmers than when equipment was shared within the community (Participant 8). Even though Amish farmers of the late twentieth century are likely to be more independent than the previous generations of Amish farmers, no Amish farmer can be or desires to be totally independent from Amish neighbors and the Amish community.

<u>Connectedness</u>. At the center of this value web is the reality of connectedness. For the Amish, all decisions are related. Where a decision leads, and not simply the decision itself, is considered important. The Amish are connected to each other -- they depend on each other as farmers, neighbors, family members and church members -- and they are connected to the land. The strong connection with the land is illustrated by the Amish belief that farming in a way which causes the soil to lose fertility is a sin as great as adultery or theft (Schwieder 1973; Hostetler 1980a). The Amish do not separate the various aspects of their existence; faith, farm and family are all connected and each depends on the other.

In Amish agriculture, the household is an essential component of a successful farm. Success on the Amish farm is not calculated by yield or profit alone. A successful Amish farm earns a profit and provides food for the family and the animals, but in addition, it protects the land, keeps the family strong, contributes to the welfare of the community and ensures the place of future generations. The ability to manage household finances wisely by limiting consumption of ready-made products and re-using and repairing possessions instead of throwing them away is an important ingredient in the successful management of the farm.

Cultural Patterns

Introduction

Today was going to be another busy day. As the warm milk squirted into the bucket between her knees, Alma hummed a happy tune. As soon as the cows were milked, the prayers said and breakfast finished, David would be off to the field to plant corn. And not long after that, the first of Alma's sisters would arrive. Today Alma was having a work day with her four sisters who lived within the settlement. Every three or four weeks all of Alma's sisters living in this community got together to work for a day. This time it was Alma's turn to have the work day at her house. The women planned to spend the day quilting, visiting and baking pies, while the children spent the day playing. Alma's mother would join them too. She and Alma's father lived in the little house connected to Alma and David's big house and were included in many family activities. Alma knew the day would be enjoyable for all of them. Being together, sharing work and sharing news was something they always looked forward to.

David was eager for his work too. The oats were all sown and now it was time to plant corn. David loved the warm sun on his back, the steady plod of the horses walking in front of him and the smell of the spring soil. While he worked, David thought about the continuous flow of the seasons. All of his life he had been surrounded and supported by a steady, dependable harmony -- on the farm and in his community. David could not imagine living without this rhythm of life.

Alma and David had been part of farm life for as long as they could remember. Both had been born in this community and now they had their own farm and were raising their own family. Just yesterday, Alma had told David how glad she was that they had been able to move to this place when her parents had retired from farming. Now Alma was able to be close to her parents and continue the farming traditions which extended back many generations, first to Ohio and now here in Iowa. David depended on her and the children; working together was the only way they could keep things going. But they also needed their neighbors.

Two days ago, on Tuesday evening, the six Amish families in David and Alma's immediate neighborhood got together to celebrate the May birthdays in their families. David, Alma and their eight children had walked the quarter mile to the Miller farm where the men gathered in the living room to catch up on farm news, the women talked and set out the food in the kitchen and the children played outside. Even during this busy planting season, there was time to be together and visit. One couldn't work in the field after dark anyway, and although everyone had worked hard all day they still had energy for visiting. The clear, calm evening was one of those rare times when nature was at its best and the world seemed nearly perfect. With the satisfaction of a day's work well done, the company of friends, a bountiful supply of freshly-baked cake and homemade ice cream, cool evening breezes and happy, contented children, what more could the world offer? At times like these David and Alma were reminded of the security, strength and satisfaction of their community of faith. They knew there would always be food on the table, a place to live and work, and family and friends to depend on. Maintaining such a community required work and sacrifice, but this was nothing new for those who were determined to remain separate from the world. Every Sunday they sang the martyr hymns which reminded them of the suffering of their ancestors. Being scorned and ridiculed were nothing compared to being imprisoned, tortured and killed. Should their faith demand it, Alma and David knew they too would be willing to suffer for their beliefs. Although they lived in the world, and had to depend on it to some extent, they did not want to allow it to completely shape their existence. They knew their decisions must be made with the good of the community in mind. These were the people who worked with them, worshipped with them and with whom they belonged.

<u>Discussion: Social organization and agriculture</u>

A striking feature of Amish society is the small, personal scale of life. Church congregations are limited to the number of families who can meet together in a home for worship, and farms are maintained on a small scale to accommodate the family and keep the community intact. Within the church, every member is known and interacts with others on a face-to-face basis. On the farm, the level of technology keeps the Amish farmer in touch with the land -- literally. The difference between riding behind a six-horse hitch and riding in an air-conditioned cab on a four-wheel-drive tractor is significant. As Kraybill (1989, 91) has observed, "the Amish realize that larger things bring specialization, distance, divisive subgroups, and often remove average people from power." In Amish society, smallness brings diversification, closeness, harmony and social equality.

<u>Diversification</u>. In mainstream society, the trend has been toward larger farms and specialized farming. Farmers now often grow only grain or raise only one kind of animal. Amish farms, on the other hand, combine crops and livestock and do so on a small scale. A typical farm will have dairy cows, horses, pigs and perhaps sheep, chickens, goats, ducks or geese. Corn, oats, alfalfa and soybeans are the major crops grown by the Amish in Iowa. In Pennsylvania, the major crops are corn, oats, rye, wheat, alfalfa and tobacco (Weidner 1988; Schneider 1986). Rotations of three or four crops combined with a variety of animals bring biological and economic diversity, spread out the risk involved in farming and result in a high level of stability.

<u>Closeness</u>. On an Amish farm, the farm family stays in close contact with nature and with each other. Milking cows together, eating together, praying together, plowing with horses, picking corn by hand, tending a garden or orchard -- all of these are reminders that one must depend on others and on the vicissitudes of nature, which are determined by God. The structure of the community encourages closeness through the proximity of Amish neighbors and the interaction of the extended family and church members. The use of horse-drawn buggies for transportation keeps people from traveling too far and the focus therefore remains on participation within the community (Larimore and Taylor 1985). The physical proximity of Amish families within the community encourages interaction (Kraybill 1989), and conversations with friends and relatives is one of the most common forms of enjoyment (Stoltzfus 1977).

<u>Harmony</u>. Within Amish society, harmony is maintained through the <u>Ordnung</u>, the set of understandings by which people in a church district

live. These common understandings, usually unwritten, result in a high degree of uniformity within the community. "A respected Ordnung generates peace, love, contentment, equality and unity" (J.F.B. 1982, 383). Unity is also evident in the shared ethnic identity of the Amish. There is room for some expression of individual tastes, but the pressure to conform to the expectations of the group is strong. Conformity is evident in language, dress, farming practices, lifestyle and religious practices. The ethnic identity, or group consciousness, "is a sense of historicity of shared biological ancestry, or inherited values and concomitant norms of behavior. This sharing comprises, in essence, a common construction of the past, the present, and the future" (Enninger 1986, 115).

Social equality. Wealth and social status are not divided equally in an Amish community, but the gap that exists between the rich and the poor in the general society is conspicuously absent in Amish society. No Amish community members do without basic needs, for example. And to an outsider, prestige and wealth are not easily identifiable. In the community itself, everyone is aware of which families are respected and which families are the most wealthy (Yoder 1989; Stoltzfus 1977), but the wealthy are not free to hoard their resources.

> The community has an informal claim on a wealthy Amishman's resources. He is also protected from an all-out competition with other well-to-do families in purchasing and displaying the usual array of material status symbols. Prestige is also culturally tied in to the welfare of the community so that personal reputation can only reach fulfillment in the service of the kin and church community. The religious support for both cultural practices is strong teaching against high mindedness or pride and a conscious cultivation of the virture of humility (Stoltzfus 1977, 312).

The strength of the community lies in its ability to maintain a system of relative equality through mutual aid and shared understandings. The Amish have found this works best in the context of small-scale, personal social organization. As a result, "the Amish dream is attainable for a much higher proportion of its dreamers than is the American dream" (Stoltzfus 1977, 313).

Summary

Amish farming systems differ in many ways from the average conventional farming system. The Amish choose to be small-scale farmers, use relatively low inputs of high technology, consistently practice crop rotation, maintain a diversified operation and base these practices on an ethic of responsibility and accountability to their religious community and to the land.

The size of Amish farms is limited by philosophy and practice. The farm is designed to be a family enterprise and also depends on close contact with other Amish farm families in the community. To maintain the strength of the family and the vitality of their close-knit community of faith, Amish farmers believe it is best to farm on a small scale. Their choice of technology reinforces this assumption. When Amish farmers farm with horses and a double-bottom plow, they cannot expand indefinitely. Family labor is also finite, and even though the Amish have large families, labor is a constraining factor.

The Old Order Amish in the study community farm with horses, milk cows by hand and limit the size, type and use of farm machinery. These practices restrict the amount of land one family can manage. In this community, an Amish farm of 160 acres is considered large (Yoder 1989), while the average farm size for Buchanan County was 254 acres in 1988 (Iowa Agricultural Statistics et al. 1989). Rather than adopting an expansionist mentality, the Amish have deliberately chosen to stay small.

A key feature of the Amish farming system is diversification. A variety of animals are always part of the farm operation and crops are always rotated. One result of crop and livestock diversification is that Amish farmers use much lower levels of external inputs than the average conventional farmer. Amish farmers use manure rather than high levels of commercial fertilizers, and they typically rely on crop rotation for primary pest control rather than using high levels of pesticides (Erb 1985; Yoder 1989). Amish farmers were quick to point out that pest problems were always greater in second-year corn and that first-year corn in the rotation had fewer pest problems. One of the reasons Amish farmers do not apply high levels of herbicides is that they must be careful to avoid carryover problems which could occur between successive crops in the rotation.

In addition to being influenced by practical concerns, Amish agricultural practices are influenced by concern for their community. The survival of the Amish community depends on the presence of many Amish farm families. While the number of farms in the general society has been decreasing and the average size increasing (Fruhling 1989; Iowa Agricultural Statistics et al. 1989), the number of Amish farms in the study community has remained nearly steady while it appears the average size has decreased.

When land prices were extremely high, some Amish farms were sold to non-Amish buyers because the Amish did not want to go into heavy debt to purchase the farms under inflated prices. However, during the "farm crisis," when land prices plummeted and farm foreclosures were an everyday occurrence, only two Amish farms, out of approximately 180, were sold. This is a loss of .01 percent, an incredible survival rate. Within the past five years, some farms have also been repurchased from the non-Amish who obtained Amish farms when land prices were high. This has kept the number of Amish farms within the community nearly steady.

When the additional land needed to start new farms is unavailable due to high prices or land shortages several options are available. Larger farms may be divided, families may double up on what land is available, new land in other areas may be purchased or new economic enterprises, such as on-farm businesses and off-farm employment, may be undertaken. For example, it is not uncommon to find two 80-acre farms where one 160-acre farm originally existed. The majority of those who pursue alternative businesses combine their pursuits with farming, but there are a few Amish families who do not farm. The most acceptable non-farm jobs are those which meet needs specific to the Amish -- buggy repair, harness making and blacksmithing, for example. Amish women also run sideline businesses such as quilt and craft shops, custom quilting and baking. All of these businesses provide additional income. Since they are home-based, they do not threaten the integrity of the family.

Rules for the appropriate use of technology are part of the Ordnung, or church rules. The rules are understood by members of the community and are usually unwritten. Breaking these guidelines may result in social ostracism, and one cannot remain a part of the community if this continues. Since the extended family, and ultimately, the Amish community, constitutes the primary frame of reference for any Amish person, being outside community boundaries leaves one without any type of social support.

Any new undertaking or innovation (for the farm or for the home) must enhance or maintain the central place of the family and protect the relationships within the community. Meyers (1983b, 76) proposes that "...as long as primary relationships continue to be within the Amish community, in addition to instrumental relationships with the English world, the community will survive." One of the functions of Amish agriculture is to preserve these community bonds (Kline 1986; Kline 1990). The Amish recognize that they must choose among options and not blindly accept anything and everything if their families, farms and communities are to remain strong and vital.

Note

1. The characters and events described in this chapter are fictitious. While they are based on the lives of real people and real events, they are not intended to resemble any particular person or situation.

CHAPTER FIVE: CONCLUSIONS AND RECOMMENDATIONS

Introduction

The initial interest in this research on Amish agriculture was prompted by the observation that small-scale Amish farmers in Iowa were relatively unaffected by the crisis in the 1980s which put other farmers, small-town businesses and rural communities at risk. In the midst of enormous economic instability, growing environmental dilemmas and social upheaval (thousands of Iowa residents moving out of the state, countless farmers being forced out of farming and rural communities faced with decay), the Old Order Amish farmers and their communities were thriving. This type of success -- keeping farm families on the farm, building the fertility of the soil for the benefit of future generations and earning a living on small holdings -- was a reality often dismissed as irrelevant in an era when agricultural leaders believed a farmer must "get big or get out." The Amish example defied this popular belief and demonstrated a viable alternative.

On the heels of the farm crisis has come the beginning of a push to examine alternative, low-input, sustainable agricultural practices. Advocates often label this a "new" movement, forgetting that a few farmers have been practicing non-conventional agriculture for many years, and that before World War II the majority of farmers in the United States used practices which could be considered alternative in the current context. The structure of agriculture has changed dramatically since the 1940s, and although many past practices may not fit today's reality, it must be recognized that alternative, low-input, sustainable agriculture is not new. Neither is it without precedent. Instead of reinventing the wheel, opportunities exist to examine the effects of alternative practices on farms that have already been using them.

Although the Amish example cannot be adopted by mainstream farmers without modification, it does offer some practical and theoretical material for consideration. The survival of low-tech Amish farms in a high-tech society is significant; it cannot be dismissed as totally irrelevant. The success of Amish agriculture is a reality.

Key Characteristics

Scale

The average size of Amish farms has remained small. In Iowa, Amish farms between 80 and 160 acres are common (Yoder 1989), while the average farm size for the state of Iowa as a whole is 313 acres (Iowa Agricultural Statistics et al. 1989). An Amish farm is small because the farm is designed to be a family operation and is labor-intensive. Maintaining small farms, instead of endlessly expanding, also ensures that the countryside in an Amish community is populated with a large number of farms. This is essential in a society where one's survival depends on the survival of the whole community. In this setting, cooperation, rather than competition, must be the focus.

Farm operation

Amish farms are diverse and employ mixed farming patterns (Erb 1985; Hostetler 1980a; Schwieder and Schwieder 1975; Yoder 1989). Along with diversified cropping systems, the Amish typically have a variety of livestock. An Amish farm typically has a few dairy cows, some pigs, beef cattle or sheep and perhaps a few goats, chickens, ducks or geese. There are also always horses, as horses are used for fieldwork and transportation. The Amish maintain large gardens for home food production and some have small orchards. The farm provides many of the basic needs for the family and the diversity and crop-animal combinations contribute to the overall stability of the farming system. Household production and its role in consumption-regulation are key components of the total operation. Small, on-farm businesses often contribute an additional source of income.

Cropping patterns

Crop rotation is an essential element of the Amish farm. The Amish used rotations in Europe and continued using them in the United States. In Iowa, two variations of a five-year rotation are the most common: two years of corn, one year of oats and two years of hay; or, one year of corn, one year of soybeans, one year of oats and two years of hay. The hay is usually cropped the first year and pastured the second year. On some farms, Amish farmers maintain permanent pasture on land which is too fragile to farm (Yoder 1989). Amish farmers can use the rotation they prefer and most suitable for their operation. Soybeans are used as a cash crop, but other crops are used on the farm as livestock feed.

External inputs

External inputs, in the form of commercial fertilizers, fossil fuels, pesticides and commercially-borrowed money are used moderately on an Amish farm. Manure from livestock on the Amish farm builds soil fertility and reduces the need for commercial fertilizer. Crop rotations reduce the need for high levels of pesticides, contribute to soil fertility and reduce the risks associated with a continuous monoculture. By discouraging excessive growth, the use of draft animals ensures the farm is operated on an appropriate scale. Their use also reduces soil compaction and keeps farm machinery investment at a moderate level. By maintaining their small tracts of land and limiting the purchase of large, expensive farm equipment, the Amish avoid huge debts. They have less need for the large loans required by many other farmers who continually expand their farm operations and purchase expensive equipment. On Amish farms, agricultural practices perform a variety of interrelated functions.

Support systems

Amish farms are operated without government assistance. The Amish do not participate in government farm programs; they depend on each other rather than on the government. As a result, their decisions are less likely to be influenced by national agricultural policy than are the decisions of a conventional farmer. Because of their religious beliefs, non-participation in war and the sufficiency of an eighth-grade, practical education for example, the Amish do not want to be obligated to the government by their participation in government assistance programs (Huntington 1956). The Amish do not accept social security and they do not carry any kind of commercial insurance. They look to their community for support from the cradle to the grave.

Underlying Beliefs

Agrarian life

From the time of their formation in Europe, the Amish have always been an agrarian people. Initially they were restricted from owning land, but instead of discouraging them from farming, this motivated them to become the best farmers possible (Getz 1946a and 1946b; Hostetler 1980a).

Their long agricultural history and the religious significance of farming are two of the primary reasons the Amish firmly believe that the agrarian way of life is the best way of life (Schwieder and Schwieder 1975; Schwieder 1973; Kline 1986).

Ethics

The religious foundation for the agrarian way of life translates into a very specific ethic of earth care. The Amish believe that farming in a way which causes the soil to lose fertility is a sin as great as adultery or theft (Schwieder 1973; Hostetler 1980a). This principle directly affects the way the Amish choose to farm. The Amish combine spiritual and environmental beliefs, and the result is a system which respects and works with nature (Stone 1989; Kline 1990). The Amish also care for their land because they want to pass it on to future generations of Amish farmers.

The community

Complementing these first two beliefs is the concern for the well-being of the community -- a group consciousness rather than an individualistic perspective -- and the practice of putting people before profits (Schneider 1986; Kline 1986; Logsdon 1986; Schwieder and Schwieder 1975). Rather than seeking to maximize profits by expansionary tactics, the Amish choose to protect the relationships within their community. Having neighbors is more important than having larger farms (Kline 1986). This belief in their community leads the Amish to make decisions outsiders cannot completely comprehend. For example, "The reason tractors aren't allowed in the fields is that they would then tempt an Amishman to expand acreage, going into steep debt to do so, and in the process drive other Amish off the land..." (Logsdon 1986, 82). The Amish recognize that their farming practices and decisions have an impact on more than the bottom line, and they are motivated by more than the bottom line. Thus, they choose carefully, so that their agricultural practices enhance the good of the group as well as the good of the land.

Indicators of Success

Stability and productivity

One of the most noticeable characteristics of an Amish farm community is the abundance of life and productivity: there are lots of people, lots of animals, many small businesses, many farm buildings and many small, productive fields. Although attempts to build new communities have not always been successful (see Luthy 1986 and Hostetler 1980b), and many new communities are small (Raber 1989; Luthy 1985), the Amish population as a whole has been growing.

As a result of the emphasis on local production, a large portion of Amish earnings remain in the community or in the local area (Yoder 1989; Logsdon 1988,1989). On the farm, much of the production is retained -- crops are fed to livestock, manure is put on the soil, garden produce is preserved and consumed by the family. This reduces the need for external inputs. On a conventional grain farm, fertilizers and pesticides are needed because manure and crop rotations are missing.

Yields within an Amish community vary, depending on management practices and weather patterns. During the drought of 1988, for example, one farmer reported that two similar fields on his 80-acre farm produced corn yields which varied more than twenty bushels per acre (Participant 10). In addition, some Amish farmers have a reputation for excelling at their occupation, while others are known for their poor farming habits.

Overall, reports indicate that Amish yields are at, or near, levels found in the general society (Logsdon 1986; Craumer 1977; Schneider 1986; Falda 1988a; Yoder 1989). The productivity of an Amish farm is not limited to or best measured by the yield of a single crop, however. Measures of productivity must also take into account livestock and milk production, long-term effects of production on natural resources (water, soil and wildlife, for example), energy consumption, overall stability of the farm operation, level of employment provided by the farm and nutrient cycling. A single-crop yield analysis simply does not tell the whole story. High yields did not save all the farmers who went out of business in the 1980s.

This study did not examine farm income, but other reports indicate that while the level of profit on an Amish farm is moderate, the profit margin is much greater than on a conventional farm (Logsdon 1988; Schneider 1986). In a good year, large-scale grain farmers may gross more money, but in a bad year they will also lose more money. The Amish farmer, on the other hand, has a more conservative level of investment and fewer expenses, so a higher proportion of the total income will be retained. The need for more and more profit does not push the Amish farmer to continually expand. In the long run, the Amish farm will have a fairly stable level of income. In one case, which may or may not be exceptional for the Amish, a young Amish farm couple had their farm paid for and a large amount of money loaned out to other Amish farmers by age 30 (Yoder 1989).

Production costs

A typical Amish farm uses a great deal of human and animal labor and a modest level of external inputs. This results in lower production costs than on a conventional farm because the Amish do not buy as much commercial fertilizer and pesticides, they do not buy large, new farm machinery and their investment in land is moderate and stays relatively stable (new land is not continually purchased or rented). The Amish have a reputation for paying cash for almost all major purchases and when they do borrow from commercial lenders it is generally at a modest level. Lower production costs and lower levels of credit reduce the chance that an Amish farmer will lose everything when times get tough.

Costs of production on an Amish farm are sometimes analyzed differently than on a conventional farm. For example, while doing a comparison of Amish and Ohio State University production costs for an acre of corn, Logsdon (1986, 82) asked his Amish source to add the cost of manure hauling in his calculations. To this, the Amish farmer replied,

> 'When I'm hauling manure, should I charge that to cleaning out the barn which keeps the cows healthy, or to fertilizing the field which reduces the fertilizer bill and adds organic matter to the soil, which in turn helps it to use soil nutrients more efficiently and soak up rain better to reduce erosion? How much do you charge for that in your computer? Or maybe I should charge manure hauling to training the young colt in the harness or giving winter exercise to the older horses. Or maybe deduct manure from machinery wear because the ground gets mellower with manure and is easier to work. I don't know how to calculate all that accurately on a farm.'

This example illustrates the multi-purpose nature of the practices on an Amish farm. The farm is not merely an economic or business enterprise, although Amish farmers have been proving their economic and business success. "Homeostasis in the Amish community, on each farm and in each field, places purpose and mechanism in subordinate roles" (Jackson 1984, 216).

Soil conservation and environmental protection

Throughout their history, the Amish have been known for their ability to build the fertility of the soil (Getz 1946a and 1946b; Kollmorgen 1942; Knopp 1946; MacMaster 1985; Hostetler 1980a). It is not uncommon for the Amish to purchase land which has been depleted by previous owners, and for them then to rebuild the fertility and productivity of the soil (Hostetler 1980b; Loomis 1979; Olshan 1980; Jackson 1988).

One of the anomalies of the Amish system is that it conserves soil and protects the environment without depending on external motivation -- higher education, county soil conservation programs or federal farm programs, for example. Based on observations in Lancaster County, Pennsylvania, Gehman (1965, 229) concluded that Amish farmers "were practicing soil conservation and crop rotation long before there were county agricultural agents." In a study in Ohio, Jackson (1988) concluded that traditional Amish farming practices have effects on the physical and chemical properties of soil, which in turn affect rates of soil loss, which cannot be predicted or accounted for by the standard universal soil loss equation (USLE). Some traditional practices used by the Amish are not even included in the standards which determine the USLE and therefore, "the tools of modern-day conservationists, such as the USLE, do not have the flexibility to account for these innovative techniques" (Jackson 1988, 485).

The exact farming practices used on Amish farms vary from community to community, as do soil types and climatic factors, so each situation will have different results. On the Amish farm, machinery use, crop-crop and crop-livestock relationships and management techniques may result in unpredictable outcomes which can only be understood by close examination and a willingness to look at details and relationships often overlooked.

The Amish and Sustainable Agriculture

Introduction

The majority of current research on Amish agriculture has not evaluated the agronomic variables of the Amish farming system. One exception to this was the study by Jackson (1988), mentioned in the previous section. Jackson's study, and other research, indicates that the complexity of the Amish system is not well represented by externally-imposed standards. To understand what is going on in Amish agriculture, one must look beyond a simple yield-per-acre analysis, for example. Yield per acre and other commonly-used standards may be misleading because they overlook factors that contribute to sustainability and are unable to take into account the interactions which occur in a multi-purpose system. These standards also overlook the long-term costs associated with a system which focuses on high yields of one crop and depends on external, non-renewable inputs.

The limitations of the Amish system

The major portion of this study has focused on the positive aspects of Amish agriculture. The Amish system is not perfect though; there are costs associated with their system. It is also true that most conventional farmers would not be willing or able to adopt many parts of the Amish system. In this section, a brief attempt will be made to point out a few of the potential drawbacks associated with the Amish system -- things the general public would have difficulty accepting.

The first thing an outsider might notice about the Amish is their high degree of internal conformity. That is, the individual is expected to conform to the desires of the group. In a system based on community solidarity and social conformity, social control must be strong and the desires of the individual must be subordinate to those of the group. People born into the Amish system must be highly socialized so their motivation to remain Amish is strong. According to Huntington (1956, 389),

> The community is very closely knit with a well-developed group consciousness and group conscience. Only the most highly socialized individuals can live the life prescribed by the Amish community. The less socialized individuals never join the church or, having joined, are expelled for reasons considered asocial by the Amish but which would be overlooked in the society at large.

The conformity demanded by Amish society is not easy for people from a highly individualistic culture to accept.

A culture with increasingly fluid role expectations would also question the rigid role expectations of Amish society. The roles for Amish men and women are clearly defined and adherence to these roles ensures the smooth functioning of the society. Clearly-defined roles serve a purpose in Amish society, but to outsiders they may appear restrictive and confining. People who do not ordinarily think of the good of the group before their own good have difficulty accepting both the level of social control within Amish society and the demands of rigorous roles. But both are necessary when the focus is on the group rather than on the individual.

Another common complaint leveled against Amish society is that decisions seem to be based solely on the desire to remain the same -- in order not to be modern. Members of Amish society are assumed to be blind to the positive aspects of modernity, unrealistic in thinking they can stop the forces of modernization and viewed as somewhat less intelligent than the rest of modern society. The philosophy behind some of the decisions in Amish society has been discussed in the previous chapter (Stoll and Stoll 1980; Kline 1986; Hostetler 1980a; Olshan 1980), but it is not clear whether the average Amish individual would have the same understanding about the reasoning behind refusing to become modern. The analyses quoted in the previous chapter come primarily from Amish leaders or Amish individuals who are exceptions in their society. It is much more common to hear that "we want to keep things the way they are" or "we don't do things that way because it is too modern." Contemporary problems in Amish society are often attributed to the fact that things are now different than they used to be. The Amish appear to assume things would be better if contemporary life was more like it was in the past (Participants 3 and 12).

Past experiences also demonstrate that the small-scale, mixed farming patterns preferred by the Old Order Amish are not able to be adapted in the same way in all parts of the United States. Very few Amish communities exist in the Great Plains, for example. Small-scale, horse-powered agriculture is not suitable for areas where it takes a large amount of land to produce an adequate income. "Amish life thrives in a moderate climate on soils reasonably fertile for general farming and livestock raising" (Hostetler 1980b, 104).

The lessons of Amish agriculture

For the Amish, a long history in agriculture, a supportive social structure and specific religious convictions have resulted in a set of agricultural practices (somewhat different in each Amish community, but based on similar principles) which encourage sustainability. Many of these practices are just as suitable for non-Amish farmers as they are for Amish farmers. The key components which have broad applicability are diversification (in crop and livestock production), crop rotations which include legumes and small grains, low external inputs (less dependence on petroleum-based products and expensive capital) and the ability to keep the role of production (outputs and growth) in proper perspective.

The Amish are successful because their lifestyle does not demand that they continually increase their consumption and their farming practices do not demand more of the land than is appropriate (Stoltzfus 1977; Logsdon 1988; LeCompte 1984; Johnson et al. 1977; Foster 1981; Yoder 1989). The Amish recognize the importance of placing certain limits on growth and consumption. This is reflected in their agricultural practices, their form of religious and social organization and their household consumption patterns. "With a sense of limitation, an individual can find balance within his social living. In agriculture this sense of limitation can act as a constraint against exploitation of his land for economic gain" (LeCompte 1984, 24-25).

It is ironic that while overproduction has led to surpluses of some agricultural products and, therefore, agricultural programs designed to take land out of production, the first argument often used against alternative agriculture is that it may decrease production (this has never been proven, however). In addition, the sole criterion often used to judge a farmer's performance is yield per acre. Strange (1988, 100) argues that

> in an age when careful use of scarce and fragile natural resources is far more important than flooding the market with food surpluses, resource consumption, not output, should be the measure of a farm. More conservation, not more production, is needed.

The Amish farming system is an excellent example of a farming system in which conservation, not overconsumption and overproduction, is the norm. The ability to limit growth and consumption must be central components of any sustainable system.

In the Amish system, scale is a crucial survival factor. A small farm and frugal consumption patterns keep financial investment at a modest level and ensure that the need for more and more profit (to repay heavy debts) does not fuel endless expansion. Conservative investment patterns protect the farm from the devastation typically caused by the extreme fluctuations of economic boom and bust cycles, and the small-scale, diversified operation spreads out the risk so that one year of crop failure will not ruin the operation as a whole. Small farms populate the countryside and in the Amish system they tend to keep profits within the local area, thus stimulating the local economy. The Amish are just one example of the long-term viability of small-scale farming. The successful small-scale family farm does not need to become a thing of the past. In fact, some studies suggest that, contrary to popular belief, small-scale farms are actually highly efficient, productive and stable (Strange 1988; Madden and Baker 1981; Schneider 1986; Logsdon 1988; LeCompte 1984). The principles at work on these farms are definitely relevant to current discussions on sustainability.

Applying the lessons of Amish agriculture

In order to reverse the destructive tendencies present in conventional agriculture, new practices, policy changes, educational efforts and a new ethical orientation must be adopted. The Amish system does not demonstrate the whole range of necessary and possible alternatives, but their farming system does illustrate some principles and practices other farmers could find useful. The Amish system is less prone to boom and bust cycles because of the limits placed on financial investment and the combination of crops and integrated crop-livestock production; the use of livestock manure, crop rotations and mechanical cultivation for weed control reduces the need for high levels of commercial fertilizers and pesticides; and these same practices contribute to soil fertility and decrease soil loss (see Jackson 1988).

A potential problem associated with applying principles and practices from the Amish experience is that in Amish society these principles and practices are supported and motivated by membership in the Amish community. Conventional farmers are typically on their own and compete with other farmers for access to land, the cleanest fields and highest yields. These farmers are often motivated by the requirements of government programs. These requirements

> have strongly encouraged farmers to specialize and deterred them from adopting diversified farming practices. ... Between the need to maintain base acres and the cross-compliance provision, farmers often face economic penalties for adopting beneficial practices, such as corn and legume or small grain rotations or strip cropping. With few exceptions, only farmers outside the programs can currently adopt these cropping systems without financial penalties (Committee on the Role of Alternative Farming 1989, 17-18, 70).

Without a supportive community and the ability or willingness to operate without government assistance, and with no government programs supporting diversification, the average conventional farmer is tied to current production systems. Changes in policy are needed to allow and encourage the adoption of alternative practices. The Amish have been able to practice a form of alternative agriculture because they are not tied to the requirements of government programs.

If conventional agriculture is to become more sustainable, changes must be tied to the adoption of a new ethical orientation. Without this ethical orientation, changes will not occur or be sustained (Leopold 1984; Deibert and Malia 1988). As long as land is seen as an input to be controlled primarily for its ability to produce profit, then profit will be the ultimate goal and it will not matter how land is treated -- as long as the practice appears profitable in the short run. The focus on profit and production tends to ignore the long-term consequences of exploitation (the long-term social and environmental costs) and overlooks the impact these consequences have on the human community. The Amish system takes into account the non-economic and cultural components of sustainability precisely because they recognize that their survival depends on both the long-term fertility of their soil and the integrity of their community. An ethical orientation recognizes the limits of the land (does not require more of the land than it can give) and strives to protect the human community both physically and socially.

It is a common assumption that the solution to almost any social problem requires more education of the public. While this is in part true, fifty years of soil conservation education has not decreased the problem of soil loss or prevented the problems of groundwater contamination. As mentioned earlier, public policy also influences agricultural practices, sometimes in ways which contradict the efforts of public education campaigns. Changes in agricultural policy and additional educational efforts, if preceded by a new ethical orientation, would begin to permit, and perhaps encourage, changes in the structure of agriculture.

Summary and Recommendations

Introduction

Although the Amish system has its weaknesses and cannot be duplicated, there are lessons to be learned and questions raised which need to be explored. The Amish example is not irrelevant. The existence of a stable and productive small, diversified farming system in an era of large, specialized agribusiness operations is significant. The Amish system does not offer solutions suitable for every situation or a perfect example, but it does make a significant contribution to the current discussion on sustainable agriculture. The Amish system, which has been in continuous use for hundreds of years, is especially relevant to current issues in the areas of agricultural research, agricultural policy and sustainable agriculture.

Research

The Amish example raises some questions and offers some new directions for agricultural research. Basic research will always have its place, but a new emphasis on farmer-centered research, using on-farm studies of alternative methods as they are currently being practiced, for example, has the potential of making the research process more relevant and of generating more appropriate and practical outcomes. Many farmers have been using alternative practices: learning from them is essential if current efforts to promote sustainable agriculture are to succeed. Farmers have a rich store of knowledge, and through their observations, researchers will be able to identify many "research opportunities" (Farrington and Martin 1987, 37). As the Amish example demonstrates, understanding the values and goals of farmers is critical to understanding their agricultural practices. The assumptions made by outsiders are often misleading; a more thorough understanding of the farming system in question will help researchers ask more relevant questions and address issues important to farmers.

Practical research, especially for application to small farms, should be a priority. In the past, this type of research has not been a priority and as a result farmers have organized themselves to carry out the research they were interested in doing (Soth 1989). Farmers themselves have always been experimenting and researchers have the opportunity to learn from their example (see Rhoades 1987; Chambers et al. 1989; Richards 1989).

Agricultural research has typically been the domain of the university and professional scientists. Because this research has often overlooked the practical concerns of farmers and has not adequately met their needs, farmers, who are practical scientists, have been organizing to do their own research. One example of this is Practical Farmers of Iowa, established in 1985 by Iowa farmers, to investigate and promote, through on-farm research, alternatives to conventional farming methods. When farmers take the initiative to do their own research, professionals should be willing to learn from them.

Instead of relying on only one research paradigm, a variety of approaches should be used. Four possible research approaches are (1) basic research done by professionals, (2) applied research controlled by professionals, (3) applied research with farmers and professionals as partners and (4) farmer-initiated, farmer-directed research with farmers controlling the agenda and professionals acting only as consultants, observers or advisors. Each approach has its place, but the last two, farmer-professional partnership and farmer-directed research, have been used so infrequently that their benefits have never been realized. Research using these approaches could offer insight based on a more thorough understanding of the farming system in question and more relevant results since the knowledge, concerns and interests of farmers would be given priority. As the Amish example demonstrates, farmers are using alternative practices researchers and other farmers can learn from. When the indigenous knowledge and experience of farmers is respected, researchers will discover that there are new ways to do research and new research priorities. Learning from farmers is an approach whose time has come.

The Amish example, as a community-oriented society, also has implications for projects and researchers at the international level, particularly for research and community development projects in small towns and rural areas. The community as a whole and the interactions which occur in such a setting, not individuals or single households, must be the focus of any undertakings in areas where social organization is based on the group rather than on the individual. Often, international research has not utilized this approach in areas where it is essential. In the case of the Amish, approaches which place primary priority on the individual, such as survey research, are not likely to be successful.

A research question which has not been adequately investigated is the differential impacts of agricultural research and policy on farms of different sizes. Research is often assumed to be scale-neutral, but Strange (1988) and Hightower (1973) suggest that when the "bigger is better" assumption guides the research process, the outcomes will naturally confirm this belief. Research designed to investigate the strengths of small-scale farms is necessary because much of the current research benefits large-scale producers (Madden and Baker 1981). The Amish example shows that small farm systems can be successful and although many people refuse to accept the evidence, a surprising number of small farms are surviving and thriving.

The Amish, and other successful farmers who use alternative practices, provide researchers with the opportunity to do research in a living laboratory. In the two oldest Amish settlements in Iowa, Amish farmers have been farming the same land for 75 to 150 years. These farms provide an excellent opportunity for researchers to investigate the long-term effects of alternative practices. This is an opportunity researchers cannot afford to miss because the Amish are using many practices currently being investigated for their application to sustainable agriculture. Interdisciplinary research conducted by male-female teams will be the most likely to reach conclusions which present a balanced view of the Amish system.

In Iowa there are Amish farmers who use small, steel-wheel tractors and Amish farmers who use horses. This provides the opportunity to study the effects each type of farming has on soil structure (see Jackson 1988). Amish farms that have been consistently using diversified crop rotations and integrated crop-livestock combinations also provide an opportunity to examine topics relevant to sustainable agriculture such as nutrient cycling; the relationships between soil structure, soil fertility and practices such as crop rotation; and the relationship between farm management practices, soil structure and soil erosion. The Amish example also provides opportunity for interdisciplinary researchers to examine the relationship between ethics and the adoption of agricultural practices. These issues are all crucial if conventional agriculture is to become more sustainable.

Policy

Previous studies have pointed out that current agricultural policy makes it difficult for farmers to adopt alternative (more sustainable) practices (Strange 1988; Committee on the Role of Alternative Farming 1989). It is also apparent that agricultural policy has different impacts on farms of different sizes. While family farming has long been "an esteemed American institution" (Adler 1989), it is often assumed that the end of this type of agriculture in inevitable (Gillete 1989). Fortunately, "if a public commitment is made, it is possible to have the kind of agriculture most of us want -- dynamic, productive, efficient, economically fair, and environmentally sound" (Strange 1988, 262). Public policy is a form of social planning and the goals chosen will be reflected in the structure of agriculture.

Past policy has helped transform agriculture into what is now commonly called agribusiness. Food and fiber production is now treated as an industrial process, not unlike that which occurs in an automobile factory, for example. The substitution of agribusiness for agriculture is a reflection of current policy, and it illustrates a mistake in logic and practice because "agriculture is not only technique. It is also, and perhaps pre-eminently, culture" (Richards 1989, 17; see also Bookchin 1976). As Wendell Berry, himself a farmer, has suggested, agriculture
> ...grows not only out of factual knowledge but out of cultural tradition; it is learned not only by precept but by example, by apprenticeship; and it requires not merely a competent knowledge of its facts and processes but also a complex set of attitudes, a certain culturally evolved stance... (1976, 20).

Until this cultural component is recognized and understood, agricultural policy will be incomplete and misdirected.

Although the Amish are not unaffected by national agricultural policy, they attempt to minimize its impact. The support they receive from their community allows them to farm without participation in government programs. (There are other farmers who do this too, however.) Their example demonstrates that with appropriate local support systems and internal motivation (the ethical orientation), alternative practices are possible. New policies are needed to make it feasible for all farmers to adopt alternative practices.

New policies can also be formed to reward new directions in research. The current focus in research is almost always on high-technology solutions. When these "industrial strength" solutions are applied, they often reduce the role of people in agriculture -- farms get bigger, there are fewer farms and there are fewer farmers. One of the concerns of policy for sustainable agriculture should be to enhance the role of people in agriculture. Sustainable agriculture should sustain family farms and rural communities in addition to the natural environment (Hassebrook 1989).

<u>Conclusion</u>

The future of rural America depends in large part upon the presence of people, and the presence of people who act in ways which protect the natural environment and sustain the human community. If farms continue to get larger, there will continue to be fewer and fewer people in the countryside. As people leave the countryside, generations of agricultural experience will be lost. The loss of this cultural knowledge will contribute to further instability because it represents a resource which will no longer be available to assist future generations of farmers. The Amish have preserved their agricultural wisdom, and it is their means of survival. This wisdom challenges the notion that unlimited growth is good for agriculture. In an Amish community, controlling growth -- by limiting the scale of farms and limiting the consumption of individuals and families -- has contributed to the vitality of the community. In Amish society, small is beautiful!

BIBLIOGRAPHY

Adler, Reid G. 1989. "Agricultural Research Policy and the Family Farm." The Ag Bioethics Forum 1(2) (January): 2.

Agar, Michael H. 1980. The Professional Stranger: An Informal Introduction to Ethnography. New York: Academic Press.

Altieri, Miguel A. 1983. Agroecology: The Scientific Basis of Alternative Agriculture. Berkeley, CA: University of California.

Anthan, George. 1989. "LISA Wins New Support." Des Moines Register 7 May, p. 1J.

Arizpe, Lourdes. 1988. "Culture in International Development." Development, Journal of the Society for International Development, Rome, Italy. (1): 17-19.

Bender, Harold S. 1934. "Some Early American Amish Mennonite Disciplines." Mennonite Quarterly Review 8(2) (April): 90-98.

Bender, Harold S. 1942. "Mennonite Origins in Europe." Number 1 in Mennonites and Their Heritage, H.S. Bender (ed.). Akron, PA: Mennonite Central Committee.

Berry, Wendell. 1976. "Where Cities and Farms Come Together." In Radical Agriculture, Richard Merrill (ed.). New York: Harper and Row.

Berry, Wendell. 1977. The Unsettling of America: Culture and Agriculture. San Francisco: Sierra Club Books.

Berry, Wendell. 1989. "Communities Must be Cherished." Des Moines Register 5 February, p. 1C.

Biggs, Mark. 1981. "Conservation Farmland Management - The Amish Family Farm versus Modern Corn Belt Agriculture." M.S. Thesis, School of Forest Resources. Pennsylvania State University, University Park.

Bookchin, Murray. 1976. "Radical Agriculture." In Radical Agriculture, Richard Merrill (ed.). New York: Harper and Row.

Brokensha, D., D.M. Warren and O. Werner (eds.). 1980. Indigenous Knowledge Systems and Development. Lanham, MD: University Press of America.

Chambers, Robert. 1983. Rural Development: Putting the Last First. Harlow: Longman.

Chambers, Robert. 1988. "Farmer First." International Agricultural Development 8(6) (Nov/Dec): 10-12.

Chambers, Robert, Arnold Pacey and Lori Ann Thrupp (eds.). 1989. *Farmer First: Farmer Innovation and Agricultural Research*. New York: The Bootstrap Press.

Christopher, Ron De. 1990. "Environment Dominating Farm Debate." *Iowa Farmer Today*, SE Edition, 27 January, p. 1.

CIKARD. 1988. *CIKARD*. CIKARD Brochure. CIKARD Center, Iowa State University. Six pages.

Committee on the Role of Alternative Farming Methods in Modern Production Agriculture, Board on Agriculture, National Research Council. 1989. *Alternative Agriculture*. Washington, DC: National Academy Press.

Craumer, Peter R. 1977. "Energy Use and Agricultural Productivity: A Comparison of Amish and Modern Agricultural Systems." M.S. Thesis. University of Wisconsin, Madison.

Cronk, Sandra Lee. 1977. "*Gelassenheit*: The Rites of the Redemptive Process in Old Order Amish and Old Order Mennonite Communities." Ph.D. Dissertation. University of Chicago, Chicago, IL.

Crowley, William K. 1978. "Old Order Settlement: Diffusion and Growth." *Annals of the Association of American Geographers* 68(2): 249-264.

Deibert, Ammertte C. and James E. Malia. 1988. "Sustainable Agriculture in Iowa: A Policy Analysis." Monograph for Public Policy Analysis, Sociology 698C. Department of Sociology, Iowa State University.

Doak, Richard. 1983. "An All-Too-Brief Return to the Joys of Life on the Farm in Years Past." *Des Moines Register* 7 September, p. 13A.

Dyck, Cornelius J. 1967. *An Introduction to Mennonite History*. Scottdale, PA: Herald Press.

Edwards, Clive A., Rattan Lal, Patrick Madden, Robert H. Miller and Gar House (eds.). 1990. *Sustainable Agricultural Systems*. Ankeny, IA: Soil and Water Conservation Society.

Enninger, Werner. 1986. "The Theme of Ethnicity in the Literature of the Old Order Amish." In *Studies on the Languages and the Verbal Behavior of the Pennsylvania Germans*, Werner Enninger (ed.). Wiesbaden: Franz Steiner Verlag.

Erb, Gene. 1985. "Amish Farmers Plow Ahead Despite Tough Times in Iowa." *Des Moines Register* 25 August, p. 1A.

Erb, Gene. 1987. "Amish vs. Chemicals: Traditional Farming in an Era of Pesticide Use." *Des Moines Register* 17 May, p. 1F.

Erb, Gene. 1988. "Amish Traditions an Ally Against Drought." *Des Moines Register* 7 August, p. 1J.

Ericksen, Eugene P., Julia P. Ericksen and John A. Hostetler. 1980. "The Cultivation of the Soil as a Moral Directive: Population Growth, Family Ties, and the Maintenance of Community Among the Old Order Amish." Rural Sociology 45(1): 49-68.

Ericksen, Julia and Gary Klein. 1981. "Women's Roles and Family Production among the Old Order Amish." Rural Sociology 46(2): 282-296.

Estep, William R. 1975. The Anabaptist Story. Revised edition. Grand Rapids, MI: William B. Eerdmans Publishing Company.

Falda, Wayne. 1988a. "Amish Shrug off Modernity, Stay Close to Old Ways." South Bend Tribune 12 March, p. 7A.

Falda, Wayne. 1988b. "Regenerative Tactics Gain Plausibility." South Bend Tribune 12 March, p. 7A.

Farrington, John and Adrienne Martin. 1987. Farmer Participatory Research: A Review of Concepts and Practices. ODI Discussion Paper 19. London: ODI.

Foster, Thomas W. 1981. "Amish Society: A Relic of the Past Could Become a Model for the Future." The Futurist (December): 33-40.

Frake, Charles O. 1964. "Notes on Queries in Ethnography." American Anthropologist 66(3): 132-145.

Frake, Charles O. 1980. Language and Cultural Description. Stanford, CA: Stanford University Press.

Francis, Charles A., Cornelia Butler Flora and Larry D. King (eds.). 1990. Sustainable Agriculture in Temperate Zones. New York: John Wiley & Sons, Inc.

Fruhling, Larry. 1989. "The 10 Tough Years that Reshaped Iowa." Des Moines Register 12 November, p. 1A.

Gehman, Richard. 1965. "Amish Folk." National Geographic 128(2) (August): 226-253.

General Assembly of Iowa. 1989. Code of Iowa: Volume II. Chapters 256 to 504B, Sections 256.1 to 504B.6. Des Moines, IA: Legislative Service Bureau, General Assembly of Iowa.

Georges, Robert A. and Michael O. Jones. 1980. People Studying People: The Human Element in Fieldwork. Berkeley, CA: University of California Press.

Getz, Jane. 1946a. "The Economic Organization and Practices of the Old Order Amish of Lancaster County, Pennsylvania." Mennonite Quarterly Review 20(1) (January): 53-80.

Getz, Jane. 1946b. "The Economic Organization and Practices of the Old Order Amish of Lancaster County, Pennsylvania." Mennonite Quarterly Review 20(2) (April): 98-127.

Gillete, Shana. 1989. "World Ag Competition May End Family Farms." Iowa State Daily 20 February, p. 2.

Gingerich, Mary Ellen. 1989. "History of the Kalona, Iowa Community." The Sugarcreek Budget 24 May, p. 2.

Gingerich, Melvin. 1939. The Mennonites in Iowa. Iowa City, IA: The State Historical Society of Iowa.

Goodenough, Ward H. 1981. Culture, Language, and Society. Menlo Park, CA: The Benjamin/Cummings Publishing Company, Inc.

Guengerich, L. Glen. 1984. Our Goodly Heritage. Kalona, IA: East Union Mennonite Church.

Guengerich, S.D. 1929. "A Brief History of the Amish Settlement in Johnson County, Iowa." Mennonite Quarterly Review 3(4) (October): 243-248.

Hassebrook, Charles. 1989. "Biotechnology, Sustainable Agriculture, and the Family Farm." Presentation at Biotechnology and Sustainable Agriculture: Policy Alternatives, 22-24 May 1989, Iowa State University, Ames, Iowa.

Hege, Christian. 1931. "The Early Anabaptists in Hesse." Mennonite Quarterly Review 5(3) (July): 157-178.

Hershberger, Guy F. 1953. "The Later Development of the Johnson County Churches." In Amish and Mennonite Church Centennial Anniversary Near Wellman and Kalona, Iowa, Compiled by Elmer G. Swartzendruber. Kalona, IA: Mennonite Historical Society of Iowa.

Hightower, Jim. 1973. Hard Tomatoes, Hard Times: A Report of the Agribusiness Accountability Project on the Failure of America's Land Grant College Complex. Cambridge, MA: Schenkman Publishing Company.

Hoard's Dairyman. 1989. "They Depend on 'On Hoof' Horsepower." Hoard's Dairyman 134(5): 187.

Hostetler, John A. 1951. "The Amish Family in Mifflin County, Pennsylvania." M.S. Thesis. Pennsylvania State College, University Park.

Hostetler, John A. 1955. "Old World Extinction and New World Survival of the Amish: A Study of Group Maintenance and Dissolution." Rural Sociology 20(3,4) (Sept-Dec): 212-219.

Hostetler, John A. 1959. "Old Order Amish." In <u>The Mennonite Encyclopedia: A Comprehensive Reference Work on the Anabaptist-Mennonite Movement</u>. Volume IV, O-Z, Supplement: 43-47. Scottdale, PA: Mennonite Publishing House.

Hostetler, John A. 1980a. <u>Amish Society</u>. Third Edition. Baltimore, MD: The Johns Hopkins University Press.

Hostetler, John A. 1980b. "The Old Order Amish on the Great Plains: A Study in Cultural Vulnerability." In <u>Ethnicity on the Great Plains</u>, Frederick C. Luebke (ed.). Lincoln, NE: University of Nebraska Press.

Hostetler, John A. 1987. "A New Look at the Old Order." <u>Rural Sociologist</u> 7(4): 278-292.

Hostetler, John A. 1989a. <u>Amish Roots: A Treasury of History, Wisdom, and Lore</u>. Baltimore, MD: The Johns Hopkins University Press.

Hostetler, John A. 1989b. "Toward Responsible Growth and Stewardship of Lancaster County's Landscape." An address to the Lancaster County Mennonite Historical Society, March 27, Metzler's Mennonite Church.

Howes, Michael and Robert Chambers. 1980. "Indigenous Technical Knowledge: Analysis, Implications and Issues." In <u>Indigenous Knowledge Systems and Development</u>, D. Brokensha, D.M. Warren and O. Werner (eds.). Lanham, MD: University Press of America.

Huntington, Abbie Gertrude Enders. 1956. "Dove at the Window: A Study of an Old Order Amish Community in Ohio." Ph.D. Dissertation. Yale University, New Haven, CT.

Iowa Agricultural Statistics, Iowa Department of Agriculture and Land Stewardship, and U.S. Department of Agriculture. 1989. <u>Iowa Agricultural Statistics 1989</u>. Des Moines, IA: Iowa Agricultural Statistics.

Iowa CCI. 1989. <u>Farming with Fewer Chemicals: A Farmer to Farmer Directory</u>. Des Moines, IA: Iowa Citizens for Community Improvement.

Iowa Legislature. 1987. House File 631, Des Moines, Iowa.

J.F.B. 1982. "Ordnung." <u>Mennonite Quarterly Review</u> 56(4) (October): 382-384.

Jackson, Mary. 1988. "Amish Agriculture and No-Till: The Hazards of Applying the USLE to Unusual Farms." <u>Journal of Soil and Water Conservation</u> 43(6): 483-486.

Jackson, Wes. 1984. "A Search for the Unifying Concept for Sustainable Agriculture." In <u>Meeting the Expectations of the Land</u>, Wes Jackson, Wendell Berry and Bruce Coleman (eds.). San Francisco: North Point Press.

Jackson, Wes. 1985. "Considerations for a Sustainable Society: The Information Implosion." <u>The Land Report</u>, The Land Institute, Salina, KS. (24): 23-24.

Jackson, Wes. 1989. "Rural America's Other Problems." <u>Des Moines Register</u> 1 October, p. 2C.

Johnson, Warren A., Victor Stoltzfus and Peter Craumer. 1977. "Energy Conservation in Amish Agriculture." <u>Science</u> 198(4315) (28 October): 373-378.

Kelley, Richard D. 1986. <u>Pesticides in Iowa's Drinking Water</u>. Iowa Department of Natural Resources Report, Des Moines, IA.

Kelley, Richard et al. n.d. <u>Pesticides in Ground Water in Iowa</u>. Study by Iowa DWAWM, IGS, UHL and USGS.

Kline, David. 1986. "No-Till Farming and its Threat to the Amish Community." <u>Festival Quarterly</u> 13(3): 7-10.

Kline, David. 1990. <u>Great Possessions: An Amish Farmer's Journal</u>. San Francisco, CA: North Point Press.

Knopp, Fred. 1946. "The Amish Know How." <u>The Farm Quarterly</u> 1(1-2): 86-132.

Kollmorgen, Walter M. 1942. "Culture of a Contemporary Rural Community: The Old Order Amish of Lancaster County, Pennsylvania." <u>Rural Life Studies:4</u>. Washington, DC: USDA, Bureau of Agricultural Economics.

Kraybill, Donald B. 1989. <u>The Riddle of Amish Culture</u>. Baltimore, MD. The Johns Hopkins University Press.

Landis, Ira D. 1945. "Mennonite Agriculture in Colonial Lancaster County, Pennsylvania." <u>Mennonite Quarterly Review</u> 19(4) (October): 254-272.

Larimore, Victoria and Michael Taylor. 1985. "The Amish: Not to be Modern." Film. Shown Sunday, 28 August 1988 on Iowa Public Television. Presented by Filmakers Library, Inc. New York, NY.

LeCompte, Peter B. 1984. "Amish Agriculture: Search for Sustainable Agriculture." Senior Thesis, Agricultural Development, Pamona College.

Leonard, Bill. 1989. "How to Clean Up Iowa's Groundwater." <u>Des Moines Register</u> 19 February, p. 1C.

Leopold, Aldo. 1984. *A Sand County Almanac, With Essays on Conservation from Round River*. *A Sand County Almanac* originally published by Oxford University Press, 1949. New York: Ballantine Books.

Leopold Center. ca.1988. *The Leopold Center for Sustainable Agriculture*. Leopold Center Brochure, Iowa State University. Six pages.

Logsdon, Gene. 1986. "Amish Economics: A Lesson for the Modern World." *Whole Earth Review* (50) (Spring): 74-82.

Logsdon, Gene. 1988. "Amish Economy." *Orion Nature Quarterly* 7(2): 22-33.

Logsdon, Gene. 1988,1989. "The Power of a Horse Drawn Economy." *Draft Horse Journal* 25(4): 5-16.

Loomis, Charles P. 1979. "A Farmhand's Diary." *Mennonite Quarterly Review* 53(3) (July): 235-256.

Lucht, Gene. 1990. "Management Practices May Improve Groundwater Quality." *Iowa Farmer Today*, SE Edition, 24 March, p. 21.

Luthy, David. 1985. *Amish Settlements Across America*. Second Printing. Aylmer, Ontario: Pathway Publishers.

Luthy, David. 1986. *The Amish in America: Settlements that Failed, 1840-1960*. Aylmer, Ontario: Pathway Publishers.

MacMaster, Richard K. 1985. *Land, Piety, Peoplehood: The Establishment of Mennonite Communities in America 1683-1790*. The Mennonite Experience in America, Volume 1. Scottdale, PA: Herald Press.

Madden, J. Patrick and Heather Tischbein Baker. 1981. *An Agenda for Small Farms Research: A Report on Phase II of the National Rural Center's Small Farms Project*. NRC Monograph. Washington, DC: The National Rural Center.

Martineau, William H. and Rhonda Sayres MacQueen. 1977. "Occupational Differentiation Among the Old Order Amish." *Rural Sociology* 42(3): 383-397.

Meyers, Thomas J. 1983a. "Amish Origins and Persistence: The Case of Agricultural Innovation." Paper presented at the Annual Meeting of the Rural Sociological Society, Lexington, Kentucky, August 17-20.

Meyers, Thomas J. 1983b. "Stress and the Amish Community in Transition." Ph.D. Thesis. Boston University, Boston, MA.

Miles, Matthew B. and A. Michael Huberman. 1984. *Qualitative Data Analysis: A Sourcebook of New Methods*. Beverly Hills, CA: SAGE Publications.

Nagata, Judith Ann. 1968. "Continuity and Change Among the Old Order Amish of Illinois." Ph.D. Thesis. University of Illinois.

Olshan, Marc A. 1980. "The Old Order Amish as a Model for Development." Ph.D. Thesis. Cornell University, Ithaca, NY.

Olshan, Marc A. 1981. "Modernity, the Folk Society, and the Old Order Amish: An Alternative Interpretation." Rural Sociology 46(2): 297-309.

Otto, J.S. and A.M. Burns III. 1981. "Traditional Agricultural Practices in the Arkansas Highlands." Journal of American Folklore 94(372): 166-187.

Pollack, Randy Beth. 1981. "Culture Change in an Amish Community." Central Issues in Anthropology 3(1): 51-67.

Powdermaker, Hortense. 1966. Stranger and Friend: The Way of an Anthropologist. New York: W.W. Norton & Company.

Practical Farmers of Iowa. ca.1988. Building Productivity, and Profitability for Iowa Farms: Practical Farmers of Iowa. PFI Brochure. Boone, IA. Six pages.

Raber, Ben J. 1989. Calender. Baltic, OH: B.J. Raber.

Redfield, Robert and W. Lloyd Warner. 1940. "Cultural Anthropology and Modern Agriculture." In Farmers in a Changing World: Yearbook of Agriculture 1940, Gove Hambidge (ed.). Washington, DC: USDA.

Reschly, Steven Dale. 1987. "From Amisch Mennoniten to Amish Mennonites: A Clarion Call in Wright County, Iowa, 1892-1910." M.A. Thesis. University of Northern Iowa, Cedar Falls, IA.

Rhoades, Robert E. 1984. Breaking New Ground: Agricultural Anthropology. Lima, Peru: International Potato Center.

Rhoades, Robert E. 1987. Farmers and Experimentation. ODI Discussion Paper 21. London: ODI.

Richards, Paul. 1985. Indigenous Agricultural Revolution: Ecology and Food Production in West Africa. Boulder, CO: Westview Press.

Richards, Paul. 1989. "Indigenous Agricultural Knowledge and International Agricultural Research." In Indigenous Knowledge Systems for Agriculture and Rural Development: The CIKARD Inaugural Lectures. Studies in Technology and Social Change, No. 13. Ames, IA: Technology and Social Change Program.

Savells, Jerry and Thomas Foster. 1987. "The Challenges and Limitations of Conducting Research Among the Old Order Amish." Explorations in Ethnic Studies 10(1): 25-36.

Schlabach, Theron F. 1988. <u>Peace, Faith, Nation: Mennonites and Amish in Nineteenth-Century America</u>. The Mennonite Experience in America, Volume 2. Scottdale, PA: Herald Press.

Schneider, Keith. 1986. "Working 80 Acres, Amish Prosper Amid Crisis." <u>New York Times</u> 28 August, p. 10I.

Schwieder, Dorothy. 1973. "Agrarian Stability in Utopian Societies: A Comparison of Economic Practices of Old Order Amish and Hutterites." In <u>Patterns and Perspectives in Iowa History</u>, Dorothy Schwieder (ed.). Ames, IA: Iowa State University Press.

Schwieder, Elmer and Dorothy Schwieder. 1975. <u>A Peculiar People: Iowa's Old Order Amish</u>. Ames, IA: Iowa State University Press.

Séguy, Jean. 1973. "Religion and Agricultural Success: The Vocational Life of the French Anabaptists from the Seventeenth to the Nineteenth Centuries." <u>Mennonite Quarterly Review</u> 47(3) (July): 179-224. Translated by Michael Shank.

Shaner, W. W., P. F. Philipp and W. R. Schmehl. 1982. <u>Farming Systems Research and Development: Guidelines for Developing Countries</u>. Boulder, CO: Westview Press.

Siewers, Alf. 1988. "For the Amish, No Life in the Fast Lane." <u>The Christian Science Monitor</u> 26 October, p. 1A.

Smith, C. Henry. 1909. <u>The Mennonites of America</u>. Scottdale, PA: Mennonite Publishing House Press.

Soil Conservation Service. 1986. <u>Losing Ground: Iowa's Soil Erosion Menace and Efforts to Combat it</u>. Des Moines, IA: USDA Soil Conservation Service.

Soth, Lauren. 1989. "Case for Sustainable Agriculture." <u>Des Moines Register</u> 8 May, p. 10A.

Spradley, James P. 1979. <u>The Ethnographic Interview</u>. New York: Holt, Rinehart and Winston.

Stayer, James M., Werner O. Packull and Klaus Deppermann. 1975. "From Monogenesis to Polygenesis: The Historical Discussion of Anabaptist Origins." <u>Mennonite Quarterly Review</u> 49(2) (April): 83-121.

Stinner, Deborah H., M. G. Paoletti and B. R. Stinner. 1989. "In Search of Traditional Farm Wisdom for a More Sustainable Agriculture: A Study of Amish Farming and Society." <u>Agriculture, Ecosystems and Environment</u> 27(1-4) (November): 77-90.

Stoll, Elmo and Mark Stoll. 1980. <u>The Pioneer Catalogue of Country Living</u>. Toronto, Canada: Personal Library Publishers.

Stoltzfus, Victor. 1973. "Amish Agriculture: Adaptive Strategies for Economic Survival of Community Life." <u>Rural Sociology</u> 38(2) (Summer): 196-206.

Stoltzfus, Victor. 1977. "Reward and Sanction: The Adaptive Continuity of Amish Life." <u>Mennonite Quarterly Review</u> 51(4) (October): 308-318.

Stone, Pat. 1989. "The Amish Answer: Environmentalism and Spirituality Part IV." <u>Mother Earth News</u> Issue 118 (July/August): 57-60.

Strange, Marty. 1988. <u>Family Farming: A New Economic Vision</u>. Lincoln, NE: University of Nebraska Press.

Sturtevant, William C. 1964. "Studies in Ethnoscience." <u>American Anthropologist</u> 66(3): 99-131.

Swartzendruber, Elmer G. 1953. <u>Amish and Mennonite Church Centennial Anniversary Near Wellman and Kalona, Iowa</u>. Kalona, IA: Mennonite Historical Society of Iowa.

Thoreau, Patrick. 1980. "On the Fringe of American Society: The Amish." PhD Dissertation, Faculte des Lettres et des Sciences Humaines. Universite D'Angers.

USDA Study Team on Organic Farming. 1980. <u>Report and Recommendations on Organic Farming</u>. Beltsville, MD: USDA.

Warren, D.M. 1989. "Editor's Notes." <u>CIKARD News</u> 1(1): 5.

Warren, D.M. and Kristin Cashman. 1988. <u>Indigenous Knowledge for Sustainable Agriculture and Rural Development</u>. Gatekeeper Series No. SA10. London: IIED.

Weidner, Krista. 1988. "They Dress the Garden." <u>Penn State Agriculture</u>. Department of Agriculture, Pennsylvania State University, University Park. (Winter): 2-11.

Wenger, John Christian. 1947. <u>Glimpses of Mennonite History and Doctrine</u>. Second Edition. Scottdale, PA: Herald Press.

Werner, Oswald and G. Mark Schoepfle. 1987. <u>Systematic Fieldwork, Volume 1: Foundations of Ethnography and Interviewing</u>. Newbury Park, CA: Sage Publications.

Yin, Robert K. 1984. <u>Case Study Research: Design and Methods</u>. Beverly Hills, CA: SAGE.

Yoder, Paton. 1979. "'Tennessee' John Stoltzfus and the Great Schism in the Amish Church, 1850-1877." <u>Pennsylvania Mennonite Heritage</u> 2(July): 17-23.

Yoder, Rhonda L. 1989. Research field notes. Department of
    Anthropology, Iowa State University.

Yutzy, Daniel. 1961. "The Changing Amish: An Intergenerational Study."
    M.A. Thesis. Ohio State University, Columbus.

LIST OF PARTICIPANTS

Participant 1. Retired Amish farmer. Buchanan County, Iowa.

Participant 2. Amish farmer. Buchanan County, Iowa.

Participant 3. Amish woman. Buchanan County, Iowa.

Participant 4. Amish businessman. Buchanan County, Iowa.

Participant 5. Amish farmer. Buchanan County, Iowa.

Participant 6. Amish woman. Buchanan County, Iowa.

Participant 7. Non-Amish farmer.

Participant 8. Retired Amish farmer. Buchanan County, Iowa.

Participant 9. Amish farmer. Buchanan County, Iowa.

Participant 10. Amish farmer. Buchanan County, Iowa.

Participant 11. Amish woman. Buchanan County, Iowa.

Participant 12. Amish woman. Buchanan County, Iowa.

Participant 13. Amish woman. Buchanan County, Iowa.

Participant 14. Amish woman. Buchanan County, Iowa.

Participant 15. Retired non-Amish farmer. Buchanan County, Iowa.

Participant 16. Amish farmwife. Buchanan County, Iowa.

Participant 17. Amish child. Buchanan County, Iowa.

Participant 18. Amish hired man. Buchanan County, Iowa.

Participant 19. Non-Amish government official. Buchanan County, Iowa.

Participant 20. Amish woman.

630.973 Y73a   94-1538
Yoder, Rhonda Lou.
Amish agriculture in Iowa

630.973 Y73a   STACKS
Yoder, Rhonda Lou/Amish agriculture in I

3 1896 00046 3590